Almost There

Elwood McQuaid with Lorna Simcox

WESTBOW
PRESS®
A DIVISION OF THOMAS NELSON
& ZONDERVAN

WestBow Press books may be ordered through booksellers or by contacting:

WestBow Press
A Division of Thomas Nelson & Zondervan
1663 Liberty Drive
Bloomington, IN 47403
www.westbowpress.com
844-714-3454

ISBN: 978-1-6642-9013-6 (sc)
ISBN: 978-1-6642-9014-3 (hc)
ISBN: 978-1-6642-9012-9 (e)

Library of Congress Control Number: 2023901047

Print information available on the last page.

WestBow Press rev. date: 02/02/2023

CONTENTS

Dedication v

Acknowledgments vii

Preface ix

Introduction xi

Chapter 1   When You're Sure You're Lost 1

Chapter 2   Welcome to Goodview 7

Chapter 3   Moving In 20

Chapter 4   Homecoming 29

Chapter 5   Possum Looking Down at Me 38

Chapter 6   With the Philosophers on Mars Hill 47

Chapter 7   There Goes the Parsonage 53

Chapter 8   Something in the Wind 60

Chapter 9   Visions of the Grim Reaper 65

Chapter 10   Goodview's Answer to the Taj Mahal 71

Chapter 11   I Think I Will 84

Chapter 12   Who Was That Masked Man? 92

Chapter 13   A Bad Day at the Outhouse 98

Chapter 14   In Pursuit of Houdini 106

Chapter 15   Mom 115

Chapter 16   Call Doctor Sam 127

Chapter 17   The Ballad of Oink McGhee 134

Chapter 18   The World Pays a Visit 139

Chapter 19   Changing Places 144

Chapter 20   Saying Goodbye 154

Chapter 21   Maxine 157

Epilogue 161

DEDICATION

For my children, who prompted me to relive our days among a wonderful people in a place and time now lost, but never to be forgotten.

ACKNOWLEDGMENTS

This book, compiled over four decades, draws from countless sources and a host of people without whom it never could have been written. My children—Tom, Andy, Melissa, and Jason—are at the top of the list, particularly Melissa (Missy), who worked tirelessly to bring this work to fruition. Their intermittent reminders, at times bordering on badgering, kept the project from remaining a promise rather than a reality.

Lorna Simcox, who has flawlessly edited everything I have written over the past several decades, was an incomparable contributor in every aspect of the making of *Almost There*. Her advice, editing, and contributions to the content of the story greatly assisted in making the book what it is. I know the enjoyment our readers discover within these pages will please her as much as it will please me.

I also am indebted to Laura Moak James, owner of Studio 2.10, Art Studio and Gallery in Lubbock, Texas, who contributed the original artwork for the cover of this book. For those wishing to make comments or inquiries regarding her services, Laura can be contacted at artstudio210@gmail.com.

To the multiple people and institutions that have taken time to search files and musty archives for photos and information, I offer a hearty thank you. Your efforts have enriched the story immensely.

I can't leave without a word for the people who will ever remain more than a story for me. Writing about you has brought me joy, and having you touch my life endures as a treasure.

Elwood McQuaid

PREFACE

The book you have in hand is about a grand passage. Not one measured by calendar years or academic proficiency, but one crafted by a stage in life that instills values and defines futures. It was a passage that transitioned my wife and me from what one might call our student, theoretical phase into one of real-world application.

For Maxine (for seventy years she embodied the "better half" of our marriage in myriad ways) and me, it was the segment of time we spent pastoring a small, rural church in Goodview, Virginia. Fresh out of university, we already had located from Michigan to the Old Dominion at the invitation of friend and classmate, Mason Cooper. Mason touted the opportunities for ministry in his home state, and his appraisal proved accurate.

Looking back at our time in Goodview today, seventy years later, I see how that once-idyllic place focused and fashioned every essential aspect of our service for Christ for the rest of our lives. And that experience is what turns this story—sketched through a host of diverse characters and vibrant situations often tinted with wisdom and humor— into a significant pattern for life.

Our story reflects life in rural America as it was in the

early 1950s. And though it follows our initiation into a lifetime of Christian ministry, it also streams beyond that element into the irredeemable alteration of America. This story represents the final page in the era of a nation of cast-off immigrants who built a country by hand and heart, fueled by the determination to make a better life in a free land for themselves and their children.

Their legacy ushered in the spectacular, industrial, mind-stunning technology that led to a new age. For the most part, these people are gone now, but they must never be forgotten. Perhaps, in some small way, a return to Goodview might help us remember them and the enormous contributions they made to this nation.

For reasons that soon will become obvious, I've changed some names and places and given pseudonyms to individuals where appropriate. However, the events are accurate, apart from the occasional embellishment an author uses to keep the narrative flowing and the readers engaged, as I hope you will be as you travel with me back to Goodview, Virginia, and to small-town America as it once was.

Elwood McQuaid
2022

INTRODUCTION

Like so much of what we cherish in life, the small hamlet tucked amid the rolling hills of rural Virginia that I write about in this book no longer exists. Goodview is still on the map, but virtually all the people I knew there more than a half century ago have packed up and gone. No longer do women with sun-leathered faces look out from their big-brimmed poke bonnets while bending over long rows of beans and collards. And you'll search in vain for men in bib overalls and high-cut brogans sauntering down the dusty lanes toting hoes or axes on their shoulders. Some of them now reside in heaven; others have slid off in the other direction.

The few still living have moved away, opting for Roanoke or similar places with strip malls and fast food. Some vaguely remember the old days and what their little community was like so long ago. Others, however, can't remember much of anything anymore.

I've decided to take a look back. If you care to, you can come along. We won't catch the local train and rumble into town with the morning newspapers and sundries, as so many folks once did. You can't do that anymore. The puffing steam engines have been replaced by growling diesels with their annoying imitations of steam whistles. Scattered railroad museums still display a few remnants of the iron horses that carried America to greatness; but seeing things in a museum is not the same either.

Nothing can compare to standing by the track when an old steel behemoth rattled by, wheezing and belching great plumes of gray smoke as it emerged from the soot-blackened tunnel at the far end of town. That experience was an exhilarating form of entertainment in the pre-television era. And the shrill dirge from the whistle of a train waiting on the siding for another train to pass excited the imaginations of children bedded down for the night.

I'm hoping these pages will transport you to Goodview as it was in the 1950s. The world then was a different place, one as foreign to people today as the horse and buggy or baggy BVDs (men's underwear). Steep hills and intimidating, winding dirt roads no longer isolate the area from the rest of the world, as they did then. Social media, instant mass communication, ribbons of rut-leveling blacktop, and cars in every garage changed the landscape.

Perhaps that is why the Goodviews of bygone America intrigue me so. The people there were originals. They didn't imitate media influencers, who have done so much to change the fabric of contemporary culture. Many were rough types, to be sure; and others were Garden Clubbers or members of the secretive Masonic Lodge and fancied themselves a cut above the rest. But most epitomized a quality of life and stability of values that have all but vanished.

Goodview blended lightheartedness with common sense, dedication, and hard work to produce an environment imbued with a sense of spirituality that still speaks to the need in each of us today. In his best-selling book, *The Greatest*

Generation, journalist Tom Brokaw made the case for the invaluable contribution made by Americans who came of age during the Great Depression and World War II. I believe he was correct. These people left an indelible imprint on our history that will never be erased or duplicated. These are the people about whom I write—the generation I miss more and more as time passes.

So come with me to Goodview, Virginia, and the values, virtues, and good life it exemplified.

CHAPTER ONE

When You're Sure You're Lost . . .

The pastor's instructions were specific. "Take [State Route] 24 out of Vinton and travel about 20 miles until you see an Esso station on the right. That will get you into Chamblissburg. Turn right there and take the road over the mountain. I can't tell you exactly how many miles it will be until you get to Goodview. But I can tell you this: Because of the way the road twists and turns, it will seem a lot farther than it is if you were doing it in a straight line."

Then with a wry smile, he added, "Just when you're sure you're lost, you're almost there."

It wouldn't be long before we discovered the reason for his smile. The pastor was Elbert Yeatts. His base for ministry: Colonial Baptist Church in Blue Ridge, Virginia. Substantial in size and influence, it bore the distinction of being the foremost, almost-unaffiliated Baptist congregation in the region. By almost unaffiliated I mean it managed to remain independent from the ubiquitous Southern Baptist Convention to which it would belong until 1962 and whose

1

denominational tentacles stretched clear across the southern part of the United States.

And though unaffiliated churches boasted no formal bishop guides, ecclesiastical oversight committees, or commissions, they still honored pastors who had earned some status and respect for being faithful to the gospel, for shepherding their congregants with compassion, and for helping and counseling other churches. In addition to these attributes, Colonial's pastor possessed a keen disposition for assisting young men entering Christian service. He offered them counsel, education, and opportunities to minister throughout the area.

Thus came our invitation to become a candidate to fill the pulpit of the Goodview Baptist Church. Our futures lay gloriously ahead of us on that pleasant spring day in 1953 as we swung onto the washboard-like gravel road that would deliver us to Goodview, Virginia. For my wife, Maxine, and me, fresh out of university and eager to test my wings, the trip was high adventure.

We lived in Roanoke, Virginia, but were both from the Midwest—flat country. I came from Michigan, where some folks looked at anything South of Toledo, Ohio, as the Deep South. Maxine came from Sumner, Illinois, a small town just beyond the Wabash River near Vincennes, Indiana. In the Midwest, roads were straight. Here in Virginia, they meandered around the base of hills with sharp cutbacks and steep grades that made you keep a tight grip on the steering wheel as you negotiated one curve after another. The drive was an eye-opening, bone-rattling introduction to what was to become our new life.

Dust boiled up from under the dashboard, which made

keeping the windows closed a bad idea. At some places, the road hugged the hillside like it was hanging on for dear life. But if you were brave enough to take your eyes off it to snatch a quick glimpse of the Virginia countryside in springtime, the hollows below treated you to a spectacular view of lush green that rambled along as far as the eye could see.

Looking down from a tight turn, we spied a small cabin emitting a plume of smoke that slowly twisted its way to the sky. Maxine said it looked like a picture you would see on a calendar. It was late March, and the chilly air still warranted firing up the wood-burning heaters. Some crops poked up from the ground. But for the most part, the farming fields consisted of long rows of rust-colored soil dug up by fall plowing, flanked by pastures already turning into rich, green carpets of color. And almost as if the hand of an artist had placed them there, small herds of red Hereford cattle bent their heads to snatch early tuffs of the green bounty.

Maxine, who could have been an accomplished artist had she not opted to become a pastor's wife, expressed a wish to sketch the scene to send back to relatives who made no secret about their misgivings concerning the Old Dominion. They felt the job I had been offered from a sizable church near Detroit fit the Lord's plan for our lives just fine. So when we told everyone at home we were heading south instead, we faced raised eyebrows and muted mutterings.

Our Midwestern family thought comic book characters like Snuffy Smith and Li'l Abner pretty much told the story of southern culture. They would learn soon enough they were as misinformed about life in the hills of Virginia as some of our soon-to-be neighbors were about people from "up North."

As we wound our way along the hills on the 28-mile drive from Roanoke to Goodview, I learned a little something more about Maxine: Her most serene moments were not when I was behind the wheel of a car. I liked to take in the scenery as I drove. After a quick look, I'd turn her way to make what I felt was an especially cogent observation, which invariably gave her a deep sense of obligation to direct operations from the passenger side of the front seat.

"You do the driving, and I'll do the looking," she insisted. It wasn't the first time I had heard those words, and it certainly wouldn't be the last.

The longer I drove, the more certain I was becoming that we somehow had made a wrong turn and were lost. Time was a factor, and it was beginning to look like we'd be late for the morning church service. I wanted to arrive in plenty of time to get acquainted with some of the leaders before I had to meet with the deacons that evening.

Soon my wife voiced her concerns, which echoed mine. Now we both wondered if we would make it to the church on time. "I'm beginning to think we missed a turn," she said. "I haven't seen any signs or indications that we're near a town. All I can see are barns and houses here and there, but for the most part, I'm looking at hills and trees. Maybe we should stop at one of these houses and ask somebody if we're on the right road."

Her words fell on deaf ears. For some inexplicable reason, I shared with millions of other males a deep disinclination to ask for directions. For the life of me, I can't explain why. I was fully aware it made no sense to wander around lost. Why not just stop and ask a simple question: "Where in the world am I?"

But asking a stranger for help somehow diminished my manhood, an attitude my brothers and I probably inherited from my father, who scorned all advice from passengers in our old Dodge sedan.

It turned out Pastor Yeatts was right. Our consternation disappeared as we drove around the bend. After a sharp turn on a steep hill, "downtown" Goodview suddenly popped into view. The little hamlet snuggled up to a depot and the tracks and siding of the Virginian Railway, a line transporting commerce to eastern Virginia and southern West Virginia. On the siding, neatly stacked alongside several flatcars, a row of pine cordwood waited to be loaded for the trip to a paper mill.

Across the tracks stood a country store, small post office, and a house we later learned was the stationmaster's residence. The only other structure of appreciable size in downtown Goodview was a tomato cannery, a mainstay of local industry that served area farmers by providing a market for their abundant tomato crops.

As we rounded the turn to the left that took us to the church, we could smell the pinesap from the cordwood spicing the air. It seemed a pleasant, fitting welcome to the place we hoped might become our new home.

Goodview Baptist Church stood on a low hill commanding a spectacular view of the area. I guessed this was probably where the people stood who first named the village. A distant woods bordered rolling alfalfa fields beginning to display the rich green hues of spring. In another direction, a herd of cattle grazed near a stately farmhouse surrounded by picturesque outbuildings. It was, indeed, a very good view.

We pulled into the church driveway, parked our car, and

with anticipation and trepidation, made our way to the white clapboard building. Waiting to welcome us stood a subdued group of parishioners. We soon learned Goodview folk restrained their enthusiasm and were not given to gushing over newcomers. They preferred to hold themselves in check until they adequately evaluated the objects of their attention.

It was then that we met Jimmie Jones.

CHAPTER TWO

Welcome to Goodview

James Jones, our first official greeter, extended a friendly hand and reassuring smile. Married with two children, Jimmie, as everyone called him, was about 10 years older than I and a veteran of World War II, where he fought on the European front. As chairman of the pulpit committee, it fell to Jimmie to explain the day's agenda.

First came the mandatory Sunday school class of about 100 people—just about every adult who attended the church. Sunday school gave the members a chance to size me up before the morning worship service, which Jimmie would conduct. He told me I could suggest hymns to complement my message, the only proviso being the church pianist had to know them. She played by ear, and if we selected something she never heard, we would find ourselves singing a cappella. The day would conclude with the Sunday evening service.

Like most young preachers, I was nervous. I knew first impressions mattered, and if I failed to make a positive one, I had little chance of rectifying it. My Sunday school lesson came from Genesis 22: In obedience to God, Abraham bound his son Isaac on an altar and was about to offer him as a sacrifice to the Lord when an angel stopped him. God had tested Abraham; Abraham passed; and for a sacrifice, God provided a ram that got caught in the bushes. It was a good lesson on faith and substitutionary atonement. So far so good.

When I paused to ask if there were questions, not a soul responded. Dead silence. It appeared the class had fallen into a collective deep freeze. That taught me my first valuable lesson about Goodview Baptists: They were not given to conversational, give-and-take-type teaching. The Socratic method was not for them. They would have rebelled against today's fashionable breakout sessions, where people freely volunteer their opinions and pool their collective ignorance. I quickly sensed the wisdom of going it solo and teaching God's Word as the Holy Spirit led me.

Following Sunday school, the deacons ushered me into a small room adjacent to the sanctuary for a preservice prayer session. Jimmie introduced the men, but the names didn't register. I was wholly absorbed trying to remember the main points of a sermon I had preached at least a dozen times. In fact, it was one of the top three in my repertoire: "The Conversion of the Philippian Jailer."

As I squinted down at my notes, they looked like hieroglyphics. I didn't recognize a thing. I concluded that prayer was something I needed desperately. At that point, it was a toss-up who needed the Lord's help more, the congregants or me. Prayer ministers to the one praying as much if not more than to those being prayed for. Talking to God calms the spirit and fills the soul. Perhaps that's one reason the apostle Paul told us, "Pray without ceasing"

(1 Th. 5:17). So I bowed my head, closed my eyes, and joined in intercession for the morning hour.

As I entered the sanctuary, the Sunday morning regulars were filling the pews. I learned later several of the more eminent among the flock, not often present at the 11 a.m. worship hour, also showed up. Although they were church members, they seldom put in an appearance. As it happened, vetting a candidate for the pulpit qualified as a special occasion, worthy of their attendance.

Heads turned when J. T. Chisom walked in. A tall, lanky, imposing figure who looked like a gentleman farmer, Mr. Chisom hailed from a prominent old family with financial interests in one of Goodview's most important sources of income, the Chisom tomato cannery. Mr. Chisom fancied himself somewhat of a tomato baron. Although he served on several church committees over the years, at this point in life his contribution to the brethren was reputed to be his vote in opposition to anything he hadn't suggested himself.

Another head-turner then entered: Miss Ellie Mae Buford. For years, Miss Ellie Mae held the esteemed position of leader of the Goodview Baptist Ladies Missionary Society. However, a few years before I arrived, she had a serious falling out with a former pastor, culminating in the Buford declaration of independence: She worked independently of church protocol and moved the monthly business of wrapping bandages and reading missionary reports from the church to the Buford home, making Miss Ellie Mae somewhat of a missionary-society matriarch in exile. Her purpose today was to check me out and ascertain whether I seemed a more pliable, accommodating sort than my predecessor.

Most of the people in the pews, however, were the

bread-and-butter worshipers who composed the nucleus of the congregation. Jimmie, a multitalented deacon, led the service. I soon learned the pianist knew all the hymns even though she couldn't read a note of music. Neither could the choir members, for that matter. But what they lacked in formal training they made up for in volume and enthusiasm. The wooden beadboard walls resonated with their pleasing tones as they sang their hearts out.

After Jimmie introduced me, I stepped up to the pulpit and launched into my well-rehearsed message. And that's when I learned a thing or two more about our great God. As I began to preach, all my notes, so fuzzy and illegible an hour ago, shone brightly from the page. Even my illustrations flowed into the basic sermon structure. God never fails to provide what we need when He calls us to do something for Him. Except for the few times Maxine winced perceptibly, things turned out well, I thought.

As the strains of that great 19th-century hymn "Just as I Am" faded and the standard handshaking ended, the deacons ushered me into a small room at the side of the platform. The time had come for the pastoral candidate grilling.

I had prepared meticulously for this moment. I had studied the Word diligently and reviewed every nuance of Scripture's major doctrines. But as the deacons of Goodview Baptist took their seats in a semicircle in the middle of the room, a queasiness overtook me. This was my first experience applying for the position of pastor, and I expected the worst. I knew that some churches put their candidates through the wringer, asking agenda-driven questions in a mean-spirited, controlling manner that almost dares you to challenge them.

It can be like facing a firing squad, and I wasn't looking forward to it.

But these men were not like that. They had not gathered to skewer me. They just wanted to make sure I was a genuine believer in Jesus Christ whom God had called into the ministry and who was committed to the clear, consistent proclamation of the gospel.

The first matter they addressed was my personal testimony: How did I become a Christian? I remembered my road to redemption vividly. I grew up in a non-Christian home, pretty much like everyone else around me in the small town of Romulus, Michigan. We were happy pagans who never went to church. One day someone invited my 10-year-old cousin Bob to Sunday school at the Baptist church. Afterward, at the dinner table, Bob informed my Uncle Howard, my father's brother, that they needed to say grace before eating.

"What's that?" Uncle Howard asked. Bob showed them. Consequently, Uncle Howard decided they all should go to the Baptist church to see what was going on over there. So, Howard and his family went and got saved. Then they invited my father, who also got saved.

By now, Maxine and I were married. That's how life was in Romulus. Almost no one went to college, and everyone married straight out of high school. I knew my father had become a believer and that Bible prophecy and the book of Revelation fascinated him because he talked about them constantly. Then I heard evangelist Hyman Appleman preach in Detroit. Billy Graham called Dr. Appleman "one of the greatest and most powerful preachers of the gospel I have ever listened to." He was right. Hyman Appleman preached clearly and eloquently, and I went home that night picturing Jesus returning in the clouds and finding me unsaved. Dr. Appleman's message made me realize my sinful position before a holy God.

The next time my father visited us and talked about Revelation, Maxine cried when he left. She had wanted to know more about the Christian faith her entire life and found herself yearning for God and assurance of salvation. "You want to be saved, don't you?" I asked.

"Yes," she replied through her tears.

"So do I." Thinking I could lead her to Christ myself, I got out an old Sunday school Bible before realizing I didn't have a clue what to do. It seemed too late at night to call my father, but I called anyway; and he came like johnny on the spot and led us both to the Lord. We got down on our knees; repented of our sins; acknowledged that Jesus bore the punishment we deserved, died in our place, and rose again; and we asked Him to forgive us and be our Savior.

I was 18. From that point on, our lives changed forever. I had peace, joy, and a love for Jesus I had never known. Nothing would be the same for us again.

When the Goodview deacons were satisfied that I was a true, born-again believer, they addressed the next matter: my call to the ministry. They wanted to make sure I didn't decide to become a minister the way some people decide to become doctors or lawyers. Preaching involves more than a personal choice of profession; it involves a God-instilled compulsion to make Christ known.

Their questions reminded me of a legendary Virginian, Civil War General Thomas "Stonewall" Jackson. Asked about his denominational preferences for the clergymen chosen to serve as chaplains under his command, the general is said to have replied, "I have no concern as to their denominational affiliation. I want just one question answered in the affirmative: Do they preach the gospel?"

In true Jacksonian fashion, the deacons regarded fidelity to the gospel as their pulpit's highest calling. They could live with whatever I lacked in maturity, judgment, and common sense. They couldn't live with a preacher who never told others how they could receive forgiveness of sin through personal faith in Jesus Christ.

Their big question was, "Will you faithfully proclaim the gospel?" Satisfied that I would, they moved on to other topics. Eventually, my commitment to the major doctrines of Scripture confirmed we were of one accord.

Then the conversation turned to Maxine. Did she share wholeheartedly in the call to serve alongside her husband as a pastor's wife? She certainly did. Maxine was my greatest asset and sincerest encourager. Wherever the Lord called me, she willingly went. When we decided to leave Michigan so I could attend Bob Jones University in South Carolina, Maxine worked the night shift in a textile mill for $1 an hour to help put me through school. Every day, she returned home exhausted just as I was leaving for class.

Money was so tight she bought bent and dented cans of food at the market because they were cheap, and she made fried baloney taste like filet mignon. In all our years together, my wife never complained about the lack of money or pressured me to ask for a raise. She made do with what we had and was happy. Yes, Maxine shared wholeheartedly in the call to serve alongside me. When I told the deacons she did, it seemed enough for these country gentlemen.

As the deacons and I filed out of the room and into the sanctuary, Maxine immediately read the relief on my face. She had enjoyed talking with the deacons' wives while I was in the meeting, but her head was filled with questions that would have to wait for answers. Jimmie said he wanted a word with us before we left for the afternoon.

"Before things go any further," he told us, "I think it's only fair for you to see the house we rent for a parsonage. It's just down the road. Follow me. This will only take a few minutes." So, Maxine and I got into our car and followed Jimmie for about half a mile.

What we found "just down the road" surprised us. Jimmie stopped in front of a ramshackle, single-story building that was so rundown I had pointed it out to Maxine when we drove by earlier, joking that we would live there if the church voted to call us. The unpainted batten board exterior screamed for attention, and the corrugated tin roof made the parsonage look more like a shed than a home.

To make things worse, the house stood so close to the dusty dirt road that we could visualize the sandstorms that would blow our way every time cars and trucks passed by. The yard fell off so sharply down a hill that pilings seven or eight feet high propped up the back of the structure. But that wasn't all. At the rear of the property, near a creek and down a hill, stood the "facility," the house's only bathroom—a relic of an outhouse that belonged to another era. Certainly not to 1953.

"I know you must be disappointed," Jimmie said, "and I don't blame you. A couple of the men who candidated here laughed and left when they saw where they were expected to live."

When we entered the house, however, things looked a bit better. All six rooms sported white paint. The living room was spacious, as was the family room; and a large dining room completed the living area. Two bedrooms occupied one end of the house. The back door opened onto a screened-in area outfitted as a laundry space, and a veranda-style porch provided a front entryway with ample room to sit with visitors in the warm summer months.

The kitchen was another story. We would not have been surprised to find a hand pump over the sink. But there was no hand pump. There was no faucet. In fact, there was no sink. There was only a galvanized bucket resting on a small table in the corner of the room.

"There's no water in the house yet," Jimmie explained apologetically. "You'll have to carry it up from the spring. But you won't have to do that for long. We've already arranged to have it piped into the house. It's just a matter of purchasing the pump and piping and having Jim install it on his day off."

Jim Thomason was the church's handyman. He worked at a furniture factory in Roanoke and knew how to do just about everything. A few years later, when a widow named Rosa had a pregnant cow that was in trouble and couldn't birth its calf, she called Jim at 2 a.m. The calf was almost her only possession. Jim called me, and we became the cow's midwives.

Jim Thomason had a heart of gold. He would do anything for anyone, never expecting anything in return. Although he never learned to read or write, no one cared because God had given Jim a gift that set him apart; and everyone trusted him.

Skeptical about getting running water into the kitchen, my wife and I looked at each other. A refined woman,

Maxine knew how to restrain her anxiety. But the thought of lugging buckets of water up from a spring multiple times a day, even for a short time, did not delight her. Jimmie probably thought he had another candidate ready to laugh and leave, so he switched to damage-control mode to try to save the situation.

"I know that's not a long-term solution," he said. "We've been talking for some time in deacons' meetings about building a new parsonage. I'm sure if the Lord calls you here, we can get started on it before too long."

Our drive back to Roanoke began in silence as both of us mulled over the events. Maxine spoke first. "How did things go in the meeting with the deacons?"

"Just fine," I replied. "They seem like a very godly, dedicated group of men. I think they would be easy to work with."

"What did they say about your salary?"

"We didn't get around to that," I answered. "I guess I should have asked them, but I just didn't think about it."

That's sort of the way it was with us. Maxine had a head for fiscal and practical matters. Salary was a fundamental issue, and Maxine asked a logical question. She could make a dollar go farther than anyone I knew. I don't know how she did it. All I know is God gave her a supernatural ability to manage money, and I depended on her completely to use that gift. She understood we worked for the Lord, and that fact was more important to us than anything we would take home in a pay envelope. Maxine took what the Lord supplied and made do.

Usually, she had $10 or less to buy an entire week's worth of groceries. One day at the market she reached into her pocket for the $10 and discovered it was gone. It had fallen out. She was devastated. But she made do without it.

On the way back to Roanoke, fiscal issues were not our primary concern. Taking the church (or not taking it) would alter our lives. If the church called us, what should we do?

The question dominated our afternoon conversation and prayers. When all was said and done, we agreed: If God called us to minister to His people at the Goodview Baptist Church, our answer would be yes.

Darkness had fallen when we arrived back in Goodview for the evening service. The nervousness I felt in the morning had disappeared, and I was calm in the pulpit. My message was tried and true: "The Three Crosses." Simple but direct, it centered on the gospel and gave people an opportunity to accept Christ as their personal Savior. The message revolved around Jesus on the cross and the two men who hung next to him. On one side was a crucified, unrepentant sinner; and on the other side was a repentant thief who said, "Lord, remember me when you come into Your kingdom" (Lk. 23:42).

I made the consequences of unbelief clear: If you die lost, without Christ, you will be in Hell without Him forever. Then I gave an altar call so people could come forward for salvation.

The evening crowd was smaller than the morning crowd, made up of the regulars, the nucleus of the congregation. These were the people who would make the final decision when the time came to vote for a pastor—something I assumed would take place a month or two down the road. For all I knew, the church wanted to hear other candidates before extending a call.

In addition, there were procedural issues. Normal Baptist protocol called for a special congregational meeting, with all members notified in writing at least two weeks before the vote. But Goodview Baptists did not stand on normal Baptist protocol. These folk were straight-line thinkers. When the evening service concluded, someone asked Maxine and me to step outside and wait in our car while the congregation took up a matter of church business.

Conversation dwindled as we sat in the dark parking lot. The clear, quiet spring night gave us a serenity that comes with being in the country, away from the city's hustle and noise. With the car windows rolled down, we inhaled the pristine freshness of the fields surrounding the church.

Then a shaft of light emerged. The church door opened, interrupting our reflection on the virtues of such a beautiful spring night. Jimmie Jones stepped out to beckon us back inside. The fact that so brief a time had elapsed did not bode well. *Perhaps the negative votes tallied up quickly,* I thought.

As we entered the church, Jimmie asked us to stand beside him on the platform as he read the results of the congregational vote. The decision was unanimous. Everyone voted yes.

We already knew what we would do. We had made our decision sitting on our living room couch in Roanoke earlier that day. We wanted to serve the Lord. And we believed the Lord wanted us to serve Him in Goodview. So we said yes. And with that simple verbal transaction, we began a new life serving God in the pastorate.

The formalities ended, and the deacons didn't waste any time putting me to work. Not ten minutes after hiring me, they informed me that as the new pastor, I now was the evangelist for the upcoming spring revival meetings. Goodview held revivals every spring and fall. Revivals were big down South in the 1950s and drew good crowds for what often was a week of church meetings designed not so much to fill heads but to change hearts.

The timing was excellent because the intervening weeks gave me a chance to settle in and prepare my sermons. The next day, I quit my temporary job in the shoe department at Sears and Roebuck in Roanoke and headed back to Goodview with my wife. We loaded our few worldly possessions onto a truck provided and driven by men of the church. I had been a terrible shoe salesman. But I was looking forward to becoming a pastor and, as Jesus said, a "fisher of men."

Maxine and I were elated. I had wondered whether mature believers in Jesus Christ, people who had walked with the Lord for years, would want to hear anything this neophyte preacher had to say. I found believers who did in rural Goodview, and I eagerly looked forward to being their shepherd. Little did I know how much they would end up shepherding me—and changing my life.

CHAPTER THREE

Moving In

With the move into our new home, Maxine and I entered a new phase of ministry for which we had little practical preparation. We were now operating in the real world, where we would face interpersonal situations unrelated to theological training.

Rural churches in those days didn't have extensive staffs. In fact, the "staff" at Goodview consisted of Maxine and me. Period. I preached, taught, visited, evangelized, headed all youth activities, organized conferences, led the congregation and choir when necessary, and handled all jobs that would end up on a honey-do-list, as necessity dictated. I never lacked for work.

And there were plenty of jobs for the pastor's wife, as well. Even today, the musically gifted (still a highly sought-after attribute in a young minister's marital search) usually fill in at the piano and organ. Although Maxine didn't play an instrument, she had a myriad of responsibilities. Most pastors' wives handled all aspects of children's activities, taught Sunday school, planned parties and church activities, served as the Women's Missionary Society leader, and participated in community activities—all while looking after their husbands' needs and, of course, rearing impeccably groomed, well-behaved children.

These tasks (and much more) were what the congregants expected of us when they voted unanimously to offer us their pulpit. And we tried not to disappoint.

High on our priority list following our move to Goodview was money. By now we had the answer to Maxine's question about salary, and it didn't bode well for family bookkeeping. I made more than two chickens a week, but not by much.

This was the early 1950s, when standards for a pastor's pay were modest and nonnegotiable. The deacons and trustees decided what the church could afford, and the figure was communicated to the prospective minister. Perks were unheard of. No one even thought to discuss travel expenses, vacation, days off, or retirement packages. Those items simply didn't exist, which was the norm in most rural churches.

"I know the Lord has called us here," Maxine told me. "But I confess, I wonder how we're going to make it on so little." This was coming from a woman experienced in making do.

My response was less than helpful. "Don't concern yourself." I said. "The Lord will make a way for us to get by." The sentiment held good for the long term, but it didn't answer the question of how we would pay our bills every month.

Little did we know what God had in store. We stepped out in faith to follow the Lord where we believed He was leading us, and we learned—as we did repeatedly throughout the years—that He is always faithful. He says in His Word,

"Call to Me, and I will answer you, and show you great and mighty things, which you do not know" (Jer. 33:3). We called, and He overwhelmed us with His magnanimous answer.

How we would make ends meet lay in the character and integrity of the people who occupied the pews at Goodview. Being the pastor made us the church's first family, so to speak; and church members believed their care for us was their unspoken responsibility. King David said, "I have been young, and now am old; yet I have not seen the righteous forsaken, nor his descendants begging bread" (Ps. 37:25). Neither would we.

Within days after we moved in, people began dropping by to fill the larder. Every day, they knocked on our door to deliver fresh produce from their gardens. Some came by just to get acquainted. Jim Thomason immediately got busy solving the water problem and installed a pump and line into the kitchen so we wouldn't have to continue hauling buckets of water up to the house from the spring. Within two weeks, our kitchen flowed with running water.

One Sunday after the morning service, as congregants filed out of the church, Mrs. Bennett asked Maxine if we liked mustard. "Yes," Maxine replied, wondering why anyone would ask such an odd question. But, occupied with greeting people, she couldn't stop to chitchat, so she let the topic slide.

That afternoon, as we rested between the morning and evening services, Maxine said, "I can't for the life of me stop thinking about Mrs. Bennett's question about mustard." That afternoon, we dozed off for a nap contemplating our preferences for various jarred mustards at the local market.

The next day, Mrs. Bennett appeared at our front door

carrying a big shopping bag. It overflowed with leafy mustard greens from her garden. "If you cook these with a ham hock or piece of pork fatback, it will make you a great meal. I love them in the spring when they're fresh out of the ground," she told us.

"I was so embarrassed," my wife exclaimed as soon as Mrs. Bennett was out the door. "My mom raised collards in her garden in Illinois, so I should have known."

When it came to greens on the table, I was not among the uninitiated. My father, an avid greens-seeker, roamed Michigan's fields after the snow and ice gave way to pick from the best of the spring dandelion invasion. His goal was to bag the dandelions before the seed bloom appeared, thus ensuring (so he told us) a more tender, flavorful morsel. For him, maybe. Not for me.

I never liked the bitter taste and grainy bits of sand that managed to hide inside the dandelions no matter how much you soaked or scrubbed them. My father's dandelions permanently diminished my enthusiasm for the leafy, "good-for-you" spring greens.

Nevertheless, Mrs. Bennett's mustard greens introduced us to an aspect of country living that bore major, practical implications. We quickly learned that most food staples were homegrown, which translated into far fewer trips to the market and far less cash outlay.

While Maxine wondered about mustard, I wondered why some of the churchmen muscled a huge chest freezer up my back stairs and onto the porch. Finances being what they were, we would never be able to buy enough food to fill it. The standard refrigerator-freezer combination more than met our needs.

My curiosity was satisfied incrementally. The good people of Goodview gave of their garden-fresh fruits and vegetables so generously we ended up with far more than we could possibly consume. Not wanting anything to spoil, we started freezing what we couldn't eat. Soon our neighbors joined in, bringing us tender young pullets for frying, some of which also ended up in the freezer.

But the biggest event that filled the freezer was the annual butchering. It took place around Thanksgiving after temperatures dropped sufficiently. Butchering was a magnificent community affair. Farmers brought their stock, mostly pork, to the sprawling Butler farm, where they took advantage of the large scalding tanks and butchering equipment that had been gathered.

The annual butchering felt like a fun-filled day at an Amish barn-raising. Folks from far and near showed up to watch the big doings, socialize, and feast on the wonderful food. Many participated in the scalding, rendering, carving, and slicing.

For this young preacher and his wife, that joyous day produced enough meat for the entire winter. We closed our freezer lid on outstanding cuts of pork and beef that we never could have afforded to buy, contributed by members of both the church and the community. When we added the meat to the already frozen vegetables, chickens, and other donated delicacies, we had food aplenty fit for a king. What the Lord wasn't giving us in money, He made up for in material goods.

God used Goodview to teach us in practical ways that He knows how to provide for those who give their lives to Him. No wonder why He tells us, "Seek ye first the kingdom of God, and his righteousness, and all these things shall be added unto you" (Mt. 6:33, KJV).

Meeting the Members

Most pastors will tell you that relationships with their parishioners don't grow in the pulpit. The pulpit is for teaching and preaching and can be a little intimidating to people in the pews. Relationships grow through fellowship, usually around dining room tables. And it was around dining tables brimming with greens, fresh-baked bread, fried chicken, ham, and favorite family desserts that we bonded with our congregation.

As we spent time in the homes of our church family, we gained insight into aspects of the rural culture into which God had placed us but about which we knew little. A window into a different type of life opened to us. We discovered, for example, that while our stint lugging buckets of water up to the house was brief, it had been a normal part of everyday life in Goodview for years—and still was for some.

We also had no idea electricity had eluded vast areas of rural America until the 1930s. Not until President Franklin Roosevelt signed the Rural Electrification Act (REA) in 1936 did the process of lighting up the farmlands gain momentum. As power lines stretched into small towns, oil lamps gave way to electric bulbs dangling from single strands of wire in homes and barns.

The REA began a revolution. The life-changing flow of electricity led to wringer washing machines appearing on porches. But considerable change came with considerable skepticism. People wondered if electricity would turn out to be a flash in the pan that would disappear without warning, leaving them in the dark—literally. So, just in case, they prepared for that eventuality, as Ron and Jill Green did.

Ron and Jill lived across the creek with their three children and were faithful members of the Goodview Baptist Church. When they invited us to share an evening meal at their home one beautiful, hot day, we were delighted. Jill was known for her sense of humor and outstanding cooking, and Ron had the reputation of being a true family man, a steady fellow you could count on as a loyal friend.

On entering the house through the kitchen, the first thing we noticed were two stoves. On one, an old-fashioned wood-burning stove, sat our dinner. On the other, a small electric stove across the room, sat nothing.

Curiosity finally got the best of Maxine, and she asked Jill why she chose to fire up the old stove, particularly on such a warm day, when she had a perfectly good electric stove a few feet away. Brushing back the beads of perspiration from her forehead, Jill replied, "Well, my mother taught me to cook on a wood stove. So I'm not really used to cooking on the electric one. I use it once in a while, but I don't like it like the wood stove. I suppose I could get the hang of it. But I wouldn't dare take a chance on messing up supper when we have guests like the preacher and his wife. Anyway, we never know out here when the electricity is going to go off. So having the wood stove, I always know I'll be able to get up a meal."

Then, with a smile, she ushered us into the living room to chat with the family while she finished up in the kitchen. For the next thirty minutes, with the wood stove going full tilt and no air conditioning, I felt like I was sitting next to a blast furnace. But when it came time to eat dinner, the old wood stove delivered the goods, just as Jill had said it would; and we became avid advocates of good old-fashioned cooking.

In a way, Jill and Ron defined Goodview and its people. They had one foot planted firmly in the past, while the other stepped ever so gingerly into the future. Many looked with skepticism at the coming of electricity and enamel-glazed stoves with baking ovens, unsure they wanted to shake hands with newfangled technology.

They did, however, shake hands with the telephone. With the installation of party-line service, a major lifestyle adjustment arrived. Cell phones, email, texting, and tweeting lay almost half a century away. In 1953 rural America, we rejoiced just to have basic telephone service. And by basic, I mean one small step up from tomato cans and string.

For starters, the party-line system didn't know the meaning of the word *privacy*. As many as ten households shared the same line. At one end of the wire were the households; at the other end was a human operator taking incoming calls and plugging callers into the desired party connection. Each household was assigned a specific number of rings. Most people knew the ring combinations of the others on their party line. So, when the phone rang, you always knew who was getting a call. And if you wanted to know what the phone call was about, all you had to do was pick up the receiver and listen. Entire conversations became fodder for community gossips.

For Maxine and me, who often ended up the recipients of "classified information," the party line became a serious annoyance. A distinct clicking sound signaled the presence of an unwanted intruder. But with no way to figure out who was listening, we guarded our speech carefully, avoiding anything gossip lovers would relish.

We guarded it, that is, when we could get the line. Some people spent an inordinate amount of their day entertaining themselves with inane chatter while others waited to use the telephone. Maxine expressed her frustration one day when I came home for lunch.

"I've been trying to get the phone all morning to call Doris and thank her for that delicious cake she left us on Sunday," she told me. "But the phone is always busy. And when I do get a chance, somebody else picks up before I can get the line. I think I'll call the phone company and complain."

"Try it if you like," I replied. "But you'd be better off— and save yourself a lot of time—by just getting in the car and driving to Doris's house to thank her in person."

Some things about country living would take getting used to. Party lines were one of them. Another was Homecoming.

CHAPTER FOUR

Homecoming

The first special meeting I preached as pastor of Goodview Baptist Church was an eight-day event leading up to one of the biggest shindigs of the year: the annual Homecoming, a huge get-together many rural and small-town southern churches still hold dear today. In 1953, the meetings constituted the official presentation of Goodview's new man in the pulpit to the larger Goodview community.

Our church attendance soared because area churches wanting to show their support sent delegations to the revival services. The guests lifted our spirits with the warmth that comes from sharing a mutual faith and an expectation of what God would accomplish during these days. They also livened things up, as did the special music provided by talented members from nearby churches. These services gave the guest pastors an opportunity to evaluate my theological depth and pulpit skills.

One of the week's premier attractions was the singing troupe that arrived with the delegation from Goodview's Green Spring Baptist Church, an African American congregation located less than a mile from us. When I left the prayer room a few minutes before the first day's service was to begin, I found the sanctuary filled to capacity.

The event even attracted nonchurchgoers who sat in their cars and pickup trucks in the parking lot, windows rolled down, anxiously awaiting the melodic strains of the Green Spring singers. They weren't disappointed.

That evening was a rousing success. The Green Spring singers' heartwarming songs of the heaven and home awaiting world-weary believers soothed and encouraged everyone. And as is so often true when the Lord is involved, the message could not have been more appropriate. I spoke on the return of Christ and the catching away (the Rapture) of His people.

What Christian doesn't want to know about those things? The apostle Paul told us we're "looking for that blessed hope, and the glorious appearing of the great God and our Savior Jesus Christ" (Ti. 2:13). One day, "the Lord himself shall descend from heaven with a shout, with the voice of the archangel, and with the trump of God: and the dead in Christ shall rise first: Then we which are alive and remain shall be caught up together with them in the clouds, to meet the Lord in the air: and so shall we ever be with the Lord" (1 Th. 4:16–17). What a day that will be! The message lifted everyone's spirits.

These annual gatherings came as close to an ecumenical alliance as you would get in rural Baptist churches in the 1950s. As I reflected on the evening after everyone went home, I felt God had accomplished something special. Not only had He blessed the message, but He made Maxine and me feel like were beginning to fit into this little community. We didn't quite belong yet, but we knew the day was coming.

We also saw the Lord change perceptions as our brothers and sisters in Christ at Green Spring and Goodview talked and worshiped together. Though the loathsome practice of segregation still plagued life in America, it didn't dominate the thinking in Goodview or deter relationships from developing. No matter their background or color, people were neighborly, cordial, respectful of one another, and dependent on one another. If someone needed help, he got it. And if someone could provide help, he gave it. Folks needed one another and took pleasure in helping one another.

The meeting set the stage wonderfully for Homecoming, the single most important day on the Goodview Baptist calendar. Everyone loved Homecoming. It brought almost all the church family—those who had moved away and those still there—together during the summer for a glorious day of reunion, preaching, afternoon festivities, music, and unbridled consumption of the best food Goodview cooks had to offer.

The rules for scheduling this big event were precise and sacrosanct, a fact I learned quickly when I suggested a date the Social Committee immediately rejected. "That simply cannot work," declared Chairwoman Martha Morgan. "We never schedule Homecoming until the pullets are old enough for frying."

Hmmm. The status of pullets. That detail never crossed my mind. It had crossed hers, however. A pro at preparing for Homecoming, Mrs. Morgan educated me on the importance of chicken maturity. The pullets were the chicks sold at the feed store in the spring, which required pampering with proper amounts of feed and yard pickings until they achieved "fryer status." Apparently, chicken maturity played a major role in any significant Baptist undertaking.

When negotiations ended and we settled on a date, I was free to mark the calendar and begin adjusting the Sunday schedule to accommodate the special event. Well, *free* may not be the most accurate word. When it came to Homecoming, the pastor deferred to the Goodview Baptist Social Committee.

"I realize, Pastor," confided Mrs. Morgan, "that you are accustomed to preaching about 40 minutes on Sunday morning, which ordinarily is fine. But on Homecoming, it might limit our time. The ladies have asked me to say that it would be best if the service ended right at noon, so the food can be put out while it's still warm."

From a pastor's point of view, the request caused a bit of consternation. After all, what was more important? Preaching or eating? I suppose it depends on whom you ask! On Homecoming, many church members brought friends and family who were far more enthusiastic about the eating than the preaching. Sometimes, they also were less than firmly rooted in the Christian faith. Some had no faith at all. Homecoming appealed to them the way Christmas and Easter did, drawing the religiously unaffiliated to put in an annual appearance at church. And though some of the regulars quietly scorned their attendance, I saw it as my one shot a year to tell these folks about Jesus and teach them His Word.

When my suggestion to begin the service at 10:30 a.m. didn't fly, I settled for the conventional 11 a.m., which everyone apparently regarded as unalterably ordained. I also learned the Social Committee's 12 noon dictum to quit preaching and stand down tolerated no exceptions.

When the big day for Homecoming finally arrived, God shone spectacular weather down on us. As Maxine and I drove to the church, we enjoyed the mild temperatures that warmed the air, with no hint of showers. All in all, prospects looked excellent for our successful introduction to a Goodview Homecoming.

As we turned in at the church, we saw the parking lot already filling up, belying the oft-stated notion that Baptists specialize in arriving just before the service begins. Church members streamed out of their vehicles, wives in the lead. Trailing behind—carrying large, food-filled baskets covered with white cloths—were the husbands rushing to get their wives' contributions to the kitchen counters and refrigerators.

Under the trees rimming the church property, men and their sons set up table after long table to prepare for the feast that would follow immediately after the service. The men also placed a few benches on the grass to accommodate the elderly and provide places where people could sit and chat with old friends and new. But most would roam from one food-laden table to another, plate in hand, sampling everything from chicken to salad to chocolate cake and enjoying one another's company.

Homecoming was a culinary World Series. It followed the season's warm-up that consisted of all those family dinners punctuated with conversations about favorite dishes and desserts. The women practiced all year for what they would bring to this big event.

As I surveyed the busy scene, I concluded that Martha Morgan and the ladies of the church were right. This was their day. I gratefully participated, but they owned the agenda, and rightly so.

I barely finished the benediction before the tablecloths were on the tables in anticipation of the feast. Maxine and I had attended our share of potluck dinners and covered-dish affairs. But we never witnessed anything like Homecoming. As we descended the steps from the sanctuary and went outside, we entered another world. Meats of all types and sizes surrounded small mountains of fried chicken at the end of each table. Platters overflowed with freshly picked vegetables and luscious greens. Big bowls of squash, cucumber, and tomato salads sat around large pots of green beans cooked for hours and flavored by ample pieces of pork.

Clearly, Kentucky Fried Chicken and Hamburger Helper would not have made the grade here. Homecoming was the one day a year no one counted calories or worried about cholesterol. All the ingredients were chosen purely for flavor; and eating to belt-loosening excess did not generate guilt, shame, or penance at the gym.

People ate with abandon from the bounty God had provided. When it came to dessert, pies and cakes of every description complemented bowls of rich banana puddings and other sweets at the end of the tables. And to top it all off was Doris Thomason's heralded coconut cake, the crown jewel at every public gathering.

Before everyone partook, Maxine and I were treated to what I learned was a time-honored tradition: the pastor's walk to view the feast. When Maxine noted that a dish of sweet pickles looked an unusual shade of green, she received a brief explanation on preparing gherkins in a copper pot, which infuses a deep emerald color to otherwise lackluster green cucumbers.

Everything was extraordinary. But if there had been a grand prize, it would have gone to Emily Watters' potato salad. Actually, the salad itself was incidental to the artwork topping it. It was the Van Gogh of potato salads. The centerpiece was a daisy sculpted from a hardboiled egg. The yellow yoke formed the center of the flower, and the white of the egg was fashioned into delicate petals. The stem and leaves were cut from the emerald-green pickles. It was a creation worthy of the Louvre in Paris. And though the first spoonful scooped from the dish seemed a desecration, hungry Homecomers soon dug in, piling the Van Gogh onto their plates along with the other specialties.

As Maxine and I began our trek around the tables, I discovered another pastoral duty that had never crossed my mind. It seemed every cook waited patiently to guide us to her contribution, prefaced by the immortal words, *You must try this.* And each one prefaced her offering with a brief history of the storied recipe handed down from generation to generation. Then it dawned on me. I was the congregation's taster-in-chief—a ministry position that demanded overconsumption. Oh Well! Pass the Van Gogh, please!

After the cleanup, the young people played games, while some of the older fellows played catch in the parking lot before the afternoon service closed the event. Although I enjoyed sports, I turned down the invitation to join in and lounged in the grass instead with the older men in their broad-brimmed hats. I liked listening to them reminisce about past Homecomings and experiences with friends who had since passed on.

I think what people loved most about Homecoming was the fellowship. They loved taking time out of their busy schedules to sit together and talk. To catch up on what was happening in the lives of those they hadn't seen in a while and to remember those they may never see again.

God in His great wisdom created us for fellowship. He didn't create us to live solitary, lonely existences. That's why death is so hard for us to bear. It separates us from our loved ones. And that's why God, also in His great wisdom, reunites us in heaven with everyone we cherished on Earth who truly was born again, "not of blood, nor of the will of the flesh, nor of the will of man, but of God" (Jn. 1:3). He fixes the problem of death that we created because of our sin. Homecoming seemed like a sweet foretaste of the good things we'll experience when we finally enter the presence of the Lord.

Three o'clock brought folks back into the sanctuary for the closing service. Special music, favorite old hymns and gospel songs, and a sermon rounded out the day. Usually, a former pastor who returned for the reunion preached. But since this was my first Homecoming and the final day of my exposure as the revival speaker, I delivered the message. Then we all said our goodbyes and left.

After the last cars pulled away, Maxine and I headed home. We entered the parsonage, closed the door, and made for the living room couch where we slumped down to rest. We had just learned what made rural living the transcending journey it was turning out to be. It had been a perfect day.

Despite all the bumps and bruises the hustle of day-to-day life brings, we experienced a true "family" gathering exuding love, at least for a day. People forgot their hurts and set aside their personal differences to enjoy this special time. "Quite a day," I commented to Maxine. "I don't think I'll ever be able to eat another bite."

"You know they were trying to please us," she said.

"Yes, I was very much aware of that. Kind of humbling, isn't it?"

"You know," she responded, "for all of the nice things they've done for us since we came to Goodview, I feel as though today we bonded with them."

"I think so too," I added.

In hindsight, I see it was a bond that would never be broken.

As my ever-perceptive wife got up from the couch and headed for the kitchen, she dispensed a bit of over-the-shoulder advice. "I think I'd hold up on that 'never be able to eat another bite' news flash. There will be tomorrow, and I'm sure you'll make a speedy recovery."

She was right, of course. And I recovered in plenty of time for the adventure that lay around the corner.

CHAPTER FIVE

Possum Looking Down at Me

Maxine thought it was a good idea.

"Go on a possum hunt? I wouldn't know the first thing about what was going on or what I'd be expected to do? I don't even own a gun. I haven't been hunting since I was a kid in Michigan and went after pheasants with my dad."

"But that's not the point," my wise wife insisted. "A number of the men Allen says will be going don't attend church. This will give you an opportunity to get acquainted with them. And you could use a night out just to have some fun with the guys."

We had been in Goodview a few months. I didn't know a lot of people; and Allen, who organized the hunt, was a good one to introduce me. He was a farmer, deacon, and a prominent member of the community. "Okay, I'll call Allen and tell him I'll go. But he'll have to explain just how you hunt possum."

When I called, Allen happily filled me in on the process. "You won't need a gun to hunt possum," he explained. "The dog does all the work. We'll just be trying to keep up with the dog."

I soon learned that dogs and hunting occupied a considerable slice of the Goodview male's schedule. For some, dogs and hunting constituted an actual enterprise. They bred dogs, trained dogs, traded dogs, sold dogs, hunted with dogs, and shared the spoils from the hunt with family and friends. A man named Lloyd, who had no other visible means of income, bred dogs exclusively for sale to local dog markets.

Allen explained that not all dogs are created equal. The Black and Tan "tree dogs" were the sophisticates among serious hunters. These tenacious coonhounds worked the creeks and hollows in search of possum, raccoon, and red fox. Their labor created a sort of business-pleasure enterprise. The hounds did the serious work, while the men enjoyed the chase.

The tree dogs sported stilted legs; long, smartly tapered bodies; and swooping, whip-like tails. Their long, bell-shaped ears dangled past soulful eyes; and no one cared that their heads fell rather short of aesthetic perfection. Lightning fast and persistent, these hounds with names that often represented their temperaments—Lady, Gus, Magic, Rusty, Lightning—seemed put on this earth to give chase, tree their quarry, and fight to the finish when the hunters finally "shook them out"—the quarry, that is.

Amazingly, the dog owners could deftly decipher every bark and yip. They could tell you in an instant which dog was making a fuss, where the barking was coming from, and what the sounds meant. Skilled coon hunters could sit in their pickup trucks, windows down, beverage of choice close at hand, and tell whether a dog was chasing, treeing, or just barking aimlessly into some underground burrow.

After a particularly good night, pride in a smart and aggressive Black and Tan stuck out all over its owner. Embellished stories of the hunt circulated around the general store's porch, the local watering hole where daily reports emanated, and dog business transpired behind the sagging porch banister. Devotees and passersby alike listened intently to dog tales. Whoppers were told and retold, and each rerun made the story considerably better than before.

Beagles held a position a step below Black and Tan tree dogs in both price and prestige. Squat and good natured, they specialized in running rabbits in large circles that eventually brought the furry creatures into the range of a single-barreled, 12-gauge blunderbuss that converted the hapless critter into dinner. Blue Tick Beagles topped the list with men who preferred to hunt while the sun was up. Possum hunting took place at night in the woods.

I liked watching the beagles. For one thing, they always seemed to enjoy themselves when they ran loose in the fields. And for another, each one had a personality all its own.

Betty was too old to hunt, but she hadn't figured that fact out yet. Scarred, with a faded pelt and deeply swayed back that caused her undercarriage to brush the grass, she labored along the track.

Younger canines showed no respect for her seniority. They obviously considered old Betty a nuisance to be barked out of the way so they could get on with the chase. While they all yapped and bellowed at every flutter of a leaf, she idled along, head down, emitting only a soft yip now and then.

Watching Betty work was a study in patience and maturity. On one occasion, when the beagles "jumped" a rabbit, the rabbit executed a cannonball-like exit from the thicket. Its flight provoked a tumultuous eruption of canine hysteria, as it rocketed along in a straight line until it put some distance between itself and its pursuers. The pack had left plodding old Betty far behind. Suddenly, the rabbit quickly cut to the right, ran a short distance, then hid in a patch of weeds.

At full throttle, the howling pack hit the spot where the rabbit executed its turn. But with ears flapping and legs pounding, the dogs kept right on going. After covering a considerable distance, they discovered they had lost the scent and milled about, yapping in utter confusion.

In the meantime, old slow Betty waddled along the track, nose to the ground, turtle-like but relentless, carefully sniffing her way toward the rabbit. When the sway-back beagle came to where the rabbit had turned, she paused, ran her head over the ground with a series of short sniffs, let out a piercing yelp, and headed straight for where the prey had holed up.

The rabbit's weed-beating departure put the young hounds on notice, and they quickly took up the chase. Again, Betty brought up the rear. That sequence repeated itself until the rabbit decided it had had enough exercise for one day and dove into a burrow, far beyond the reach of its frantic adversaries.

As I watched Beagle Betty, I couldn't help but think of King Solomon's admonition in the book of Ecclesiastes: "The race is not to the swift, nor the battle to the strong, nor bread to the wise, nor riches to men of understanding, nor favor to men of skill; but time and chance happen to them all" (9:11). Just because people may be old and plodding, it's best not to count them out because you never know how God might decide to use them.

I also discovered a moral in all of this—a lesson from Betty: Enthusiasm and energy may take you a long way, but not always in the right direction. Better to slow down and make sure you wind up in the right place.

I was in the right place as I prepared for my first foray into the shaded woods in search of wily creatures of the night. The right place was the spacious Morgan farmhouse kitchen. Despite the late hour, Lewis Morgan's mother, Cora, and her two teenaged daughters bustled around preparing a feast for the 15 of us. Cora controlled the proceedings, and her aproned girls hustled to obey her every command.

Seeing it was the new preacher's inaugural night out with the boys, Cora deemed the occasion worthy of a sumptuous sendoff. The aroma of hot, strong coffee wafted through the air, and a large table in the middle of the kitchen looked like the annual spread for a team of wheat thrashers. Fried chicken, sausage, eggs, biscuits large enough to fill a hand, and every condiment you could possibly want lay within easy reach.

"Better eat up, preacher," Lewis laughed. "You'll need it before the night is through." I soon learned this bit of advice came from a man who knew what he was talking about.

Helen

Our hound was somewhat of a Goodview celebrity. Her name was Helen, and where it came from was anybody's guess. Helen's owner, Uncle William (though he was no one's uncle that I know of), got her as a puppy and picked the name from some fragment of his past that he chose to keep to himself.

Known as an unrelenting, one-of-a-kind tracker of game

over any type of terrain in any type of weather, day or night, Helen was so good Uncle William refused to sell her for any amount of money even though he was virtually penniless and could have made a bundle on her.

The man was too old and physically debilitated to work, except for an occasional odd job here and there. But he was a gentleman, with a quiet dignity about him.

His wife, Lena, had passed away years before both of their sons, Luther and Leon, died in the war. Luther succumbed in the jungles of the Pacific during World War II, and Leon was killed in the European campaign. With no known family, the old man's only companion was his Helen. They had an unbreakable bond. Sometimes I'd see them walking slowly along the road, side-by-side, spending what was left of their lives together.

Uncle William was too old and infirm to hunt. But Helen wasn't. Yet William didn't loan Helen to just anyone. He granted that privilege to a favored few, and among that few was Lewis Morgan. Lewis and William often passed the time together talking crops and enjoying William's tales of bygone days. So William trusted Lewis with Helen. In return, any quarry Lewis bagged or shot during the hunt he laid at William's door.

Bagging the Beast

After we consumed the last draft of coffee around Cora Morgan's table, we filed out of the farmhouse and into the night, walking toward a gate that opened on the large pasture bordering the dark wooded area where the hunt would take place.

Guided only by the pale glow of the rising moon spilling across the field, we found a grassy spot at the edge of the woods to sit and wait for the action to begin. As I surveyed the group, I divided them into two packs: the younger guys who looked ready to run full throttle at Helen's first yip, and the older guys who would walk awhile then stop to determine if something significant was about to happen or if the dog had "treed" the quarry and the shake-out could begin.

Fancying myself a member of pack number one, I took off at top speed when Lewis yelled that he thought Helen was onto something. What I failed to reckon with was that these men all knew the lay of the land, even in the dark. They knew the ruts, the holes, the trip hazards. I knew nothing. And that deficiency in knowledge was precisely why I ran headlong into a three-strand barbed wire fence; flew over it into a brier-infested creek; and emerged bloody, brier-raked, wet, and—needless to say—humiliated.

Jimmie Jones was the first to shine a light on me and survey the damage. "Are you all right?" he asked.

I wasn't, but I sure wasn't going to tell him that.

"I know it's dark out here," he said, "so just stay close to me, and you'll be okay."

The remainder of the night was pretty much a repeat of the first couple of hours, minus my humiliation. Starts and stops punctuated our time as we waited affirmation from Helen that she finally had one where she wanted it.

When we arrived at the scene, the hound was standing on her back paws looking up at a pair of eyes shining from the light of Lewis's lantern. "Who wants to go up and get him?" Lewis asked.

"This is a small tree," Lee answered.

"Maybe if we all shake it, we can get him down."

We did, and the possum fell to the ground. "Who has the bag?" Lewis asked.

"I've got one," said Ned as he pulled a burlap bag out of his pocket. So, bag in hand, Lewis picked up the unresisting possum by the tail, dropped him into the bag, tied the top, and that was that.

"That's it?" I asked.

"Yup, that's it."

"This wasn't a good night," someone said. "We usually bag three or four. We'll do better next time."

As the group began to disperse and we all headed back to the cars, I couldn't help but think that Maxine had been right. Possum hunting wasn't my thing. But it didn't matter. The experience provided a great time to bond with some of the younger church members and get acquainted with others I hadn't met, reminding me yet again that relationships aren't forged in the pulpit. They're forged through fellowship, and fellowship can have many faces.

Tonight, it looked a bit like Helen, whose hunting acumen helped connect me with members of my congregation. As I approached the front door, Maxine was there to greet me.

"Why aren't you in bed?" I asked.

"I couldn't sleep much thinking about you out in the woods all night. I was beginning to think I shouldn't have insisted that you go." Surveying the vestiges of my humiliation, she declared, "Oh, sweetheart! You look awful! Let me get you coffee and something warm to eat."

"No. Really, I feel fine. All I need is a warm bath and some time in bed." As I slipped beneath the clean sheets and warm cover, I couldn't help thinking, *McQuaid, you need to*

*work on giving your wife honest answers when she asks you how
you feel.*

Then I thought about something else: the "we'll do better next time" comment. Hmmmm. *They'll do better next time,* I thought. I fell asleep confident my possum-hunting days were over.

CHAPTER SIX

With the Philosophers on Mars Hill

Goodview's main centers of community influence resided in three institutions. Material matters of great consequence were deliberated at the train-depot desk of the cigar-crunching station master, Amos Henry. Spiritual issues were addressed up the hill at the church. And issues associated with the more mundane stuff of life were hashed over at the general store, a business that dominated a prime piece of real estate at town center.

Proprietors Sam and Bonnie Johnson catered to the needs of locals by stocking an eclectic assortment of groceries, hard goods, and millinery products in the tradition of the mom-and-pop stores that serviced so many small towns before the carnivorous superstores and dot.com vendors made them relics of the past.

For generations, Sam and Bonnie's was where customer and proprietor addressed each other by their first names and where people took time to talk, share community gossip, catch up on family news, and discuss things of little consequence that rubbed some of the dull off their day-to-day routines.

Cash sales were meager. Instead, most people ran lines of credit. Bonnie, in charge of the bookkeeping, recorded each customer's charges in little books she stored in wooden cheese boxes stacked behind the cash register. When payday arrived, her customers showed up at the store. She told them how much they owed, and they'd settle accounts. It was an unsophisticated system, but it worked.

These mom-and-pop establishments made people feel that individuals mattered. The community was rooted in a mutual interdependence that bound souls together. No one needed seminars and lectures on how to be caring and benevolent because regard for their neighbors' needs permeated their genes.

Had someone introduced a "random act of kindness" campaign the likes of which we sometimes see today, people would have been incredulous. Dispensing kindness was not a random act; it was the expected thing to do. The "me" generation that is so obsessed with self-aggrandizement had not yet been born. These folks could be defined by a "we," rather than a "me," mentality.

For all the action that took place daily inside Goodview's general mercantile, more actually transpired outside on the porch. Early in the week, locals made their way to the store in anticipation of the train's arrival from Roanoke. It dropped off the mail and the morning edition of *The Roanoke Times* before getting up steam to move on toward the next stop on the local route.

Within the pages of the *Times* came news from a world away. When I first joined the early morning assembly occupying the benches and lining the porch steps at the Johnsons' general store, I remembered a scene from the book of Acts where the apostle Paul deliberated with the philosophers on Mars Hill in ancient Athens. Admittedly, far lesser matters were examined on the porch. Though conversations in Goodview didn't aspire to the Athenian level of contempt for those with conflicting opinions, and the loose planks of the Johnson portico couldn't match the dignity of the stone-crested hill made famous by the apostle's presence, the abundance of daily news still stirred emotions and provided fodder for animated exchanges.

Much of the conversation in 1953 related to news regarding President Harry S. Truman's departure from the Oval Office. In January, the feisty ex-commander-in-chief dropped the mantle of the presidency of the United States of America onto the shoulders of General Dwight (Ike) David Eisenhower, former supreme commander of the Allied Forces in Europe during World War II.

Spicing up the political conversation was the gossip-column flavor of the exchanges between Ike and Truman during the transition. For starters, Truman, a Democrat, was dismayed that the general, whom he counted a close friend during the war in Europe, had committed the ultimate betrayal by running as a Republican. Consequently, the transfer of power turned into a contentious free-for-all by the time the January inauguration took place. So much so that Truman called Ike a coward, to which the president-elect snarled that he wondered if he even "could sit next to the guy" for the traditional limousine ride to the ceremony.

Adding to the fracas was Eisenhower's refusal to join the ex-president for the customary cup of coffee inside the White House before entering the limo. Instead, he waited in the limousine. Truman retaliated by refusing for a while to go out to the vehicle altogether.

All this took place while America's ears still rang with the repercussions of Truman's unceremonious firing of the idolized American general, Douglas MacArthur. The Korean War (1950–1953) was raging when Harry S. sent MacArthur packing despite the fact the general's exploits in the Pacific theater during World War II made him a hero. Some even thought of him "as very much the American Caesar." One observer went so far as to exclaim, "Americans looked on him as a kind of god." President Truman didn't share the opinion.

Truman's reputation slid downhill over other issues as well. As one journalist commented 50 years later, "Harry S. Truman left office in 1953 a failure, his administration seemingly undone by the Korean War, rumors of Communists in the government and corruption in several federal agencies. In his waning days in office, the public bestowed on him a dismal approval rating of 23 percent."[1]

But even after Mr. Truman's tenure expired, he still had not become old news. And he certainly wasn't old news to the occupants of the Johnsons' portico in the spring of 1953. The men I sat among did not share the dismal assessment of the departed commander-in-chief.

One morning in particular taught me a lesson I've never forgotten. The conversation on national affairs became my introduction to lively rhetorical exchanges of opinion. Young and not yet seasoned in the delicate art of ministerial diplomacy, I learned at the feet of the men at Goodview that sometimes the wisest move is to keep your opinions to yourself. It's important to recognize when silence is truly golden.

The morning gatherings were passionately Democrat. Unbeknown to me, a Midwestern observer unschooled in local ways, contrary opinions were not welcome when political discussions were afoot—especially the highly charged emotional ones over the Republican invasion of the Oval Office.

My family were staunch Republicans. So much so, that my father winced at comments that approved of the late President Franklin Roosevelt and what Dad perceived as the follies of the Democrats' New Deal. My father never hesitated to express his disdain in political diatribes against Roosevelt's successor, Harry S. Truman—opinions he justified based on Truman's early association with the notoriously corrupt Kansas City, Missouri, political machine run by boss Tom Pendergast.

My verbal misstep of the morning came when I offered an opinion contrary to the collective sentiment on the porch. A few frosty glances shot my way, followed by a crisp comment from the postmaster, which sent a message loud and clear: "You don't bite the hand that feeds you."

The apostle Paul had walked through a marketplace filled with artifacts of cults, pagan altars, and an altar erected "to the unknown God" (Acts 17:23). That altar represented the sum of confusion and spiritual deprivation surrounding him, and the Athenians' lost condition minted his message. In the marketplace, in the synagogue, and with the philosophers on the hill—in essence, to Jews, Gentiles, Greeks, and whoever chose to listen—Paul preached the Good News of Jesus and His resurrection.

That was the imperative of his message. It was also to be the imperative of mine. And I didn't want to jeopardize my opportunities to talk about what truly matters in life—the destiny of our eternal souls—for the sake of sharing a few words on less important subjects.

The writer of Proverbs said, "There is one who speaks like the piercings of a sword, but the tongue of the wise promotes health" (12:18). God had called me to promote spiritual health, and I learned not to trade that privilege for a few briefs moments of spouting my opinion. Each of us is entitled to personal preferences and points of view, but I learned it was best to keep mine on irrelevant matters to myself.

As I descended the Johnsons' version of the Athenian hill, words from King Solomon the wise inscribed in Ecclesiastes came to mind: There is "a time to keep silence, and a time to speak" (3:7). I'd remember that in the future.

1   Christopher Shea, "Think Tank; About Harry Truman, the Jury's Out (Again), *The New York Times*, nytimes.com, December 21, 2002.

CHAPTER SEVEN

There Goes the Parsonage

For the most part, Goodviewans lived by a simple philosophy: Promises made are promises kept. The congregation promised a young pastor and his wife that it would build them a suitable parsonage; and a few months after we arrived, the people at Goodview Baptist Church officially voted to keep that promise and appointed the church trustees to oversee the project.

Following the meeting that approved the undertaking, Clovis Anthony, the committee chairman, sat down with Maxine and me to discuss our preferences. My response was to defer to Maxine, who immediately provided a word sketch of the basics for housing, entertaining, and providing for guests. Being able to house visiting preachers, missionaries, and others was essential because the day of putting them up in hotels and serving restaurant fare had not yet arrived. In fact, the majority of parishioners would have disliked the suggestion that we not entertain guests in homes, where they could enjoy hearty home-cooked meals and the warmth of a family atmosphere.

Clovis concluded by saying he would order several books of plans for us to look over so we could decide on something suitable, and he would bring our choice to the trustees for their approval at their next meeting.

Slamming the Door

Things seemed to be going well as the trustees took their seats around a long table where the plans we had chosen were spread out. The meeting was just getting underway when a late arrival entered the room. It was the station master, Amos Henry, who also happened to be a trustee and the powerful owner of one of the town's three canneries.

On most occasions, Mr. Henry was a member in absentia. So he was not expected to be at this meeting—but there he was. And he got right to the point. "Let me have a look at those plans," he said. As he eyed them slowly, page after page, he began to shake his head.

"No, no," he said. "These will never do. I don't approve them. I'll get something together and get back to you."

Clovis and his fellow trustees were stunned. "But the pastor and his wife settled on this plan, and we are in agreement," he stammered.

"Well, I'm not!" Amos shot back. "And if you go ahead with this, I'll have nothing to do with it." That said, he stormed out of the room.

Somewhere in the world a door may have slammed shut with more force than the one that Amos slammed shut that Thursday night. But I don't know of it. For a few moments, a silent pall hung over the room. Then, in an almost inaudible voice, trustee Tut Jones muttered, "There goes the parsonage."

Maxine and I were crestfallen. This was unbelievable. Everyone was so confident about building the house. How could one individual scrap the entire project?

What we did not know was how dependent the Goodview community was on Mr. Amos Henry. Without his resources, influence, and equipment, the project would suffer a huge setback.

A Second Opinion

Chairman Clovis's departing word that night told us not to rush to a gloomy conclusion. There would be a joint meeting of the deacons and trustees following the Sunday evening service, and we should wait until we heard from them.

When the meeting took place, it seemed excessively long. Small talk with the deacons' wives did little to calm our anxiety. Finally, the door opened, and I was invited into the room. Grayson Thomas, chairman of the deacon board, spoke for the group.

"We've decided, in spite of what took place in the trustees meeting, to go ahead with building the new parsonage. That was, after all, the decision of the congregation. And we think it only right to proceed. We'd like you and Mrs. McQuaid to look into where you feel is the best place to build."

We could have told him on the spot. Maxine and I felt for a while the best property for a parsonage lay right across the church driveway. A large oak tree stood there, and we often sat by it in the evening as the smell of honeysuckle filled the air and a magnificent view of the sunset-lit fields spread out before us.

But God doesn't always make things easy. He puts

obstacles in our paths so that we must depend on Him. I soon found out there was a problem, the magnitude of which was explained to us by the chairman. Matthew Evans owned the land we needed; and apparently, he wasn't about to sell it to us. "We've made several attempts to buy land for expansion from Matthew, but his answer is always the same. He will not sell property to the church," Grayson Thomas said.

"But all of the family, including his mother, attend," I said.

"That's true, but this goes back a long way when he fell out with the church and one of the former preachers, and he has never forgotten or forgiven what happened."

At the inaugural meeting of the building committee (the deacons and trustees anointed with a new title), the foremost issue was where to build. Again, I tried to make the case that the best spot was the ground adjacent to the church property.

The response was nearly universal: That was not possible. Nevertheless, the faint whiff of "maybe" still hung in the air.

One old-timer quickly expressed his skepticism. "We'd be wasting our time to expect to buy any land from Matt Evans. He's told us before that none of his land is for sale, and it never will be—especially to the church. People like him have long memories, and he's not likely to change his mind."

Perhaps it was because these men did not wish to dash the dream of their young pastor and his wife that they opted to make one more go at it. The question was how to make the approach.

Clovis suggested a three-member committee be appointed to visit Mr. Evans as representatives of the congregation. Grayson was unimpressed with the idea. "We did that several years ago, when we last wanted to make him an offer for land. We hardly got through the door when he said no. I think the best thing to do is to have the pastor himself go and make the offer. The family likes him. Perhaps he'll listen to him."

All hands willingly gave that plan their approval. I wasn't so sure the go-it-alone method was to my liking, and I had little enthusiasm for it. A little handwringing in front of Maxine did nothing to persuade her to console me. "I think it's the right idea," she said. "Who better than you to explain why the land is needed?"

Her straightforward, to-the-point reasoning wilted my resolve. Resistance seemed futile.

Daniel or Don Quixote?

The meeting was set for the following Thursday evening at 8, which meant there would be little warm-up conversation before we faced off on the issue.

As I prepared to leave the house, Maxine fiddled with my tie while she offered a parting comment. "Remember that I'll be praying for you, and you speak up and let him know just how badly we need the land. What I don't understand is why some of the men on the committee aren't going with you. They've known him for years. It seems logical to me that they should go too. If you want my opinion, I think they're afraid."

Maybe they were. I don't know. I do know that I had to go it alone. Matthew's wife, Emma, met me at the door with a pleasant smile. "We've been waiting for you. Matthew is in the living room. Follow me."

She ushered me in, exited the room, and closed the door behind her—an action that didn't seem to bode well for what was about to take place.

Small talk in a frigid atmosphere is a problem for most folks. For a young preacher who hadn't been on many excursions into the proverbial lion's den, it was excruciating. Most difficult was broaching the subject of the land purchase. I didn't relish bringing it up. How could I get down to the business at hand? It was well known in the community that Matthew was not long on small talk. On this warmish evening, he lived up to that characterization.

We exchanged pleasantries about weather conditions for hay bailing and other incidentals that held little, if any, interest to either of us. As the time ticked by, I experienced a rather strange sensation. I felt like I was in one of the western movies I'd seen as a boy: two men facing each other on a dusty street at high noon. Who would be the first to draw? It would be Mr. Evans.

"I think I know why you've come. They're planning to build a parsonage, and the church wants to buy a piece of my land to put it on. Well, I'll tell you straight out, just what I've told them time and time again. I will not sell a piece of my land to the church for any price they offer."

Talk about having the wind knocked out of your sails. This was it. I hadn't uttered one word on the topic and the conversation appeared over.

"I won't sell it, Reverend," he said. "But I'll tell you what I will do. Meet me up there in the morning and we'll stake off as much as you need. I won't charge a cent."

I was stunned. *This can't be happening,* I thought. I was

caught in a surge of disbelief. Was my overstressed mind playing games on me?

It wasn't. Matthew Evans meant exactly what he said. And when I finally pulled myself together to thank him and say that the church was willing to pay for any land he might consent to sell, the man was firm.

"I meant what I said. There will be no charge for the land. Years ago, my family gave the land the church stands on as a gift. And even though I don't attend any longer, I feel I cannot do less than they did. And you can tell that to the men on the board."

I've learned over the years that God loves a miracle. He loves to do the seemingly impossible to bless His children who have faith in Him. He loves doing "exceedingly abundantly above all that we ask or think, according to the power that works in us" (Eph. 3:20).

People say we must never underestimate the power of prayer. I think it more accurate to say we must never underestimate the God who answers prayer if what we want is within His will. And apparently, that year, He wanted a parsonage for Goodview Baptist Church. But we would soon learn that the miracle He performed to procure the land was only the beginning.

CHAPTER EIGHT

Something in the Wind

As soon as I stepped through the door, the expression on my face told Maxine what happened in the Evanses' living room. "He decided to sell!" she exclaimed. "How much is he asking? Are you sure he means it?"

"I'll tell you everything. But first I need to call Clovis so he can get in touch with the others. He's not going to believe what happened."

I was right. The chairman's first words were, "You wouldn't joke about this, would you?" When he heard the details, he immediately got off the phone so he could tell the others. "I've got to call the men and tell them the news!" he said excitedly.

As Maxine and I sat together and talked about how the Lord had answered prayer and what a new home would mean to us, we had no idea how profoundly Mr. Evans's gift would affect the community as well. Something was in the wind; a change was coming in ways no one could have anticipated.

Since the infamous Amos Henry door-slamming incident, opinions had been mixed as to whether the parsonage project could ever get off the ground. The acquisition of land, however, brought material substance to the endeavor. There was land for the house. And the fact that it was acquired after the community's top man had announced his disapproval set tongues wagging at every stop in the village.

Clearly, the land issue, coupled with the congregation's decision to proceed with the project, brought a type of David-versus-Goliath scenario to Goodview. Goodview Baptist's young pastor had, in a few minutes during a single visit, managed to accomplish what dozens of others had not. As a result, people stopped criticizing me behind my back. The snickering at my youth and inexperience began to fade, and my stature as a leader rose dramatically. Interestingly, all these changes transpired without my having to utter a single word. To me, it seemed that my most significant achievement was showing up for the meeting. But it didn't seem that way to everyone else.

Looking back on the situation today, I realize God was elevating the man of His choosing despite my youth. He was showing His hand of blessing and solidifying my call to the pulpit of Goodview.

The invisible hand of God also was engineering other circumstances behind the scenes. He says in the book of Isaiah, "I work, and who will reverse it?" (43:13). The answer, of course, is no one. When God wants something, He gets it. Evidently, He wanted the parsonage, and He provided for it in a way that would alter life in the small village.

A major portion of Goodview's residents were indebted to Amos Henry, the community patriarch. In many ways, he was like the fictional Boss Hogg of Hazzard County. Everyone needed his help with something. Some carried short-term loans with him, others needed his financing to purchase land or sell their tomato crops. Even a job loading cordwood onto rail cars for shipment to the paper mill required a dispensation from the man behind the station desk.

Not surprisingly, when someone felt he had been taken advantage of, he kept quiet about it, rather than stand up for himself. Whether justified or not, people felt they might pay the price if they raised Amos's ire by saying too much.

No one disliked the station master or wished to plot some evil form of revenge on the man. The decision to go it alone regarding the parsonage really said more about the men of Goodview than about Amos Henry. They needed to affirm their independence and sense of self-respect—to restore their personal dignity, so to speak. They were going to make a statement that would produce material evidence of their worth and position in the village. And that fact became evident when our phone began ringing.

Lining Up

"This is Ben, Pastor. I heard about Matthew giving land for the parsonage and have something you may want to think about. As you know, I'm not wealthy and won't be able to contribute money for the building. But I do have a woods full of trees. Plenty of them are good-sized oak and pine that would provide more than enough lumber for the house. I'll donate the trees if you can find enough men to cut them and haul them to the mill."

Finding men to cut and haul trees was not a tall order in Goodview. Chainsaws were ubiquitous. Politicians were promising a car in every garage, but we could guarantee a chainsaw in every shed.

In practically no time, Clovis called to say he had rounded up a crew that would be in Ben's woods on Saturday morning to cut the trees. And he had another bit of news that came as a shocker. "I've gone to see Jubal, who owns the sawmill, to find out how much he'll charge to saw the lumber," Clovis said. "He told me if we haul the logs to the mill and provide the men to work with him, he'll do the job for free. All we have to do is buy the gas for the mill."

Jubal Yancey's offer stunned me. Even though his wife, Caroline, and their girls regularly attended church, Jubal was a hard nut to crack. He steadfastly turned the other way when spiritual issues came up. All business, he never showed a proclivity for anything to do with the Goodview Baptist Church.

Trees Coming Down

"So, you're going to be a lumberjack!" my wife said when I rigged up and prepared to head for Ben's woods on Saturday morning. "You don't know anything about sawing down trees. You're apt to get yourself killed if you don't watch out."

"You don't know all there is to know about me," I teased, even though she probably did. We had known each other since high school. In fact, the principal had her tutor me through ninth-grade algebra so I could continue playing football. Not much about me was a mystery to Maxine.

"I have experience in the business of felling trees," I protested.

"Well, you never told me about it," she replied.

I never told her because there wasn't much to tell. My father, an avid gardener, decided one day to chop down a small tree growing too close to his vegetable patch. Seeking someone to man the other end of the crosscut saw, the instrument that would get the job done, his eyes fell on the only prospect standing in the area: me. I was probably 10 years old. My older brother, Walter, quickly saw the handwriting on the wall and made himself scarce. So I got the job.

Crosscut saws can't hold a candle to chainsaws, but the chainsaw was still a tool of the future. The crosscut saw we used was a wobbly 5-footer with long vertical handles on either end. Today these saws decorate the walls of rustic-style restaurants that love to use antiques.

Unfortunately, the crosscut saw made it easy to perpetrate two transgressions while subduing a tree, both of which I evidently committed because I frequently heard about it at a loud pitch during my brief initiation into lumbering.

"Quit riding the saw!" my father complained. That was the dominant offense. To this day, I can find no definition as to how one rides a saw. "Don't push the saw when I'm pulling!" That was the other offense I heard about throughout that sweaty day.

It seemed like it took my dad and me forever to fell the tree; and by the time we finished, and I was savoring a cool glass of Mom's tea, I had already concluded that lumberjacking was not the occupation for me.

Now I was going to be back at it. *God, grant me the strength,* I said to myself. It would take only a few days in the sawdust at Goodview to again confirm the determination of my youth. But those few days became part of the miracle of the Goodview parsonage.

CHAPTER NINE

Visions of the Grim Reaper

Maxine was as apprehensive about my lending a hand at the sawmill as she had been about my possum hunting in the woods. Consequently, she treated me to a hearty breakfast and some words of caution to guide me as I set out on my day in the sawdust.

"Eat up. It will be a long time before lunch, and you'll need your strength. Above all, be careful. Remember, you're a preacher, not a logger. And I'm told that a sawmill is a very dangerous place to work. I want you back here in one piece. So watch your step, and let the men who know what they're doing be in charge."

Before I made it outside, Maxine was waving me back. She had answered a telephone call; and with her hand clasped tightly over the mouthpiece, she whispered, "You'll never guess who it is. It's Amos Henry at the depot!"

As I took the call, I wondered what I would hear. We hadn't spoken since the night he announced his dissatisfaction at the trustees meeting and slammed the door behind him. Perhaps he would thrash me with a diatribe telling me he considered my conduct inappropriate and that I hadn't learned my place. Or worse, maybe he was getting ready to charge me with ministerial malfeasance for leaving the study for the sawmill. Or maybe he called to tell me he was initiating a move to oust me from the pulpit altogether.

To my surprise, there was no conversation, just one sentence delivered in a somber tone. "Stop by my office on your way out this morning."

Suddenly, I felt the same eerie anxiety that seized me when I approached Matthew Evans's house to plead for a piece of land. The gruff-voiced station agent impressed me as a tough character from the movies, an old Edward G. Robinson type. A shortish man, he usually sat hunched over a desk piled high with papers he might get to someday. Hanging from the side of his mouth was the ever-present stub of a stogie that had run out of fire but was still serviceable and waiting to be rekindled.

Amos Henry was not known for mincing words or spouting pleasantries, and he didn't violate his reputation that morning. "I understand Ben has given the church some oaks and other trees for roughing in the new parsonage, and you all will be at Jubal's today sawing up the logs," he said.

"Yes sir," I replied. "I'm on my way there now."

"Well, Preacher, you know how I feel about the church going ahead with the house against my advice. And I can tell you, I'm still not happy about it. But since Evans gave the land, Ben the trees, and Jubal is going to saw the logs, you're going to need trucks to haul the wood to the mill in Stewartsville. You know I have several trucks and other pieces of equipment you'll need after the building gets started. As soon as you need a truck, call me; and I'll send one over."

That was it. I took a stab at saying thanks and telling him how much the men would appreciate his help, only to have him wave me away. I imagined Amos had come as close as he ever would to saying uncle. It was as though the day of miracles had unexpectedly dawned in Goodview.

God had just parted the Red Sea. I had been worried my career at Goodview might be over; and instead, the Lord strengthened it. His deliverance that day didn't involve the high drama of 3,000 years ago, when He piled up the waters and brought the Israelites fleeing Egypt through the Red Sea on dry shod. But it was a miracle just the same.

Moses had told God's people, "Do not be afraid. Stand still, and see the salvation of the LORD, which He will accomplish for you today" (Ex. 14:13). I stood still, and God did the rest.

When I broke the news to the men at the sawmill, it invigorated them with the force of a tsunami. That Amos Henry was cooperating confirmed the fact that something much larger was happening here than simply building a house. Differences still existed, of course. But when it came to the subject of a parsonage for the pastor and his wife, a unity had formed; and it was binding us together.

Eyeballing My End in the Sawdust

It was high entertainment in Goodview in those days to spend a day at the sawmill when Jubal Yancey was at the top of his game turning logs into lumber.

Watching huge lengths of timber turned into 8 x 10 sleepers, 2 x 4 studs, and 1 x 6 sheathing was witnessing a craftsman in total control of his skill. Though many men in town could multitask, only Jubal knew how to eyeball, manipulate, roll, and run the unwieldy giant hulks of oak and other species into manageable, cut-to-order building wood and cabinetry material.

The master of the tiller on the huge, circular saw that sliced through wood like a knife through warm butter was not a man given to idle conversation or social amenities. The father of five attractive daughters, he expended a considerable amount of energy simply trying to ward off unworthy suitors—which, now that I think of it, may have produced his constant need for Maalox. He took so many of the antacid tablets that the corners of his mouth always bore their traces.

Jubal's wife, Caroline, was a devout woman who worked in the furniture factory in Roanoke. She spent her Sundays creating sumptuous meals for her family and attending services at the church. Her Sunday morning ritual always included inviting her husband to accompany her to hear the pastor's message. No one could quite calculate the number of times her husband fabricated ways to say, "Not today." But I'm sure it was impressive.

On the days Jubal cranked up the motor on the mill, onlookers always showed up. That was nothing unusual. What was unusual the day I showed up was the inordinate number of onlookers. The parsonage project had become the talk of the town, and people vied for position to get a look at the goings-on.

I was front and center when assignments were distributed for the day's cutting. Since I had no experience in the industry, I got the post of an off bearer, which meant I was one of the men who carried off the freshly sawed wood and stacked it in piles prepared for drying before it would be taken to the lumber yard for finishing.

Damp wood is heavy. I quickly became aware of that fact as I muscled the first 2 x 10 from the saw to the growing stack of oak piles. As the day wore on, I began to feel twinges of distress in my legs, telling me I probably needed to sit down. It was then I noticed some of the spectators whispering to one another. I suspected they were guessing how long the pastor would last before he quit lugging lumber.

Their skepticism reflected a common opinion among working men: They held a dim view of ministerial commitment to manual labor. According to their calculations, a pastor only worked one day a week. And even then, the heaviest thing he lifted was a hymnal.

Most people have no inkling how hard a pastor works. Much more goes into running a church and shepherding a flock than preaching on Sundays. Some pastors become so stressed out and overworked they get sick or leave the ministry.

So, as far as I was concerned, the gauntlet was down. In the flying sawdust of Jubal Yancey's sawmill, I intended to put to rest the notion that this pastor couldn't handle physical labor. At first, it went well. But as the day wore on, I began wishing old Jubal would slow the pace and allow for some breathers. But he was a man on a mission who wanted to take the straightest possible road to the finish line, so he kept that saw blade spinning.

Before long, the situation turned grim. I was nearing exhaustion, and the men watching began to wonder how long I could last. Assessing the situation, John, a member of the church, stepped over with an offer. "Let me take your place for awhile," he suggested.

There are times when a man's common sense and rational faculties fail him. This was such a time. I could describe it as bravado over brain or a temporary breakdown. No matter, I waved John away. "No thanks, I'm just fine," I told him, which, of course, I was not. But grim determination drove me to prove a point. Preachers, with some exceptions, are not slackers when it comes to hard work. And I validated myself before the skeptics in the gallery.

Still, there are times when the best sound that comes is no sound at all. On this day, under layers of sawdust and sweat as I gasped for the next breath, I heard the whine of the motor turning the blade begin to die. It was over! The last log had been subdued and reduced to serviceable dimensions.

For Goodview's young pastor, it was a stellar moment. Far more had gone down that day than the Dr. Pepper I held in my blistered hand. I felt I had looked the grim reaper in the eye and survived. I fought the good fight, I finished the race, I kept the faith. I didn't sit on the sidelines. I got into the trenches, proving to myself as much as to anyone else that, with God's help, I could stay the course.

CHAPTER TEN

Goodview's Answer to the Taj Mahal

Patience is not a trait common to most young Americans. Whether we're preparing for Christmas, birthdays, sports events, or more intensely emotional milestones such as marriage, we are a species bundled with repressed anxiety, yearning for the day to arrive when things get started.

After Amos Henry's trucks pulled away from the sawmill and headed to the lumber-milling plant where the wood would be cured and finished (and I had recovered from those dreadful hours of agony in the sawdust), I became afflicted by the let's-get-going syndrome.

On the ministerial front, things were functioning pretty much as usual. In addition to the daily summer gab fests on the porch of the Johnsons' store, people gathered inside around a pot-bellied, wood-burning stove when the weather turned bad. It was raining when I pulled opened the screen door that day. No sooner had I stepped foot into the building than I was greeted by "Here he is! Let him settle this!"

By now, the Goodview collective regarded me as the theologian in residence. That day, the verbal fracas at the mercantile generated so much heat there was no need for the stove. Everyone held on tightly to his decidedly immovable opinion on the subject under discussion, which was the eternal security of born-again believers in Jesus Christ.

William Jeffry, an old-line Methodist, held to the Armenian position, declaring, among other things, that the grace of God is not irresistible; and one can fall from grace (lose his salvation). Alvin Phillips led the argument for the Calvinist point of view: God's grace is irresistible; and once someone is saved by grace through faith in Christ, he or she is saved forever (perseverance of the saints).

As the appointed arbiter of this theological skirmish, I was acutely aware there could be no victory. Whatever I said would anger somebody and, most likely, not influence anybody. The conflict was more about combat than conclusion.

No sooner had I begun my explanation of the conflicting strains of theology than Fred Dillon called out, "Why don't you ask William if you can lose your salvation by not showing up for church? I can tell you that I haven't seen his face there for more Sundays than I can count."

That was enough for William. "I don't have time for any more of this," he said sourly. "I've got things to do." And with that, he turned abruptly and left the store.

I love teaching God's Word. But few things are more aggravating than trying to explain something to people who don't want to listen and have no intentions of changing their minds no matter what you tell them. I could have thanked Fred for terminating what might have been a long, indecisive stand-off. Like William, I had things to do. We were about to begin the initial stage of building our new home.

It was a beautiful day when I pulled up to the building

site. *Perfect,* I thought, *to begin the grand adventure of putting a parsonage on the hill.* This was the country, not the city; and when I got to the spot where the foundation was to be dug, a group of early risers already stood assembled waiting for things to begin.

These days people put great stock in preconstruction groundbreaking ceremonies, where men and women don plastic hard hats and scoop small shovels of dirt while grinning into a photographer's camera. Such ostentatious displays would have made for amusing conversation on the Johnsons' porch.

These people viewed labor from another perspective entirely. Putting shovels in the dirt did not require ceremonial niceties. All they needed was instructions on who should follow which marker of lines for the foundation, and the work began. They were ready to put their hands to the plow and not look back.

Dad Is on the Way

My father was a man who relished a challenge. In many respects self-educated and ambitious, he managed to advance from being a sheet metal worker at the Stinson Aircraft Company in Wayne, Michigan, to the position of chief inspector for a major American aircraft producer during the war.

While his profession was putting planes in the air, his delight was carpentry. On his days off he roamed all over the community laying walkways or hammering nails into some structure his builder friends were erecting. There wasn't a plethora of housing developments or subdivisions in the

1950s, and many people built their own homes. Battery-powered wonder tools were years away—merely a thought in the minds of inventors.

Thus, Dad learned construction from the ground up at his own initiative. The crowning achievement of his spare-time projects was a small home he built for our family that took us from a rental on Bibbins Street in Romulus, Michigan, to a debt-free bungalow in the country.

When the church finalized its decision to build a parsonage, Dad wanted to know every detail about when construction would begin and how he could become involved. "Send me a copy of the plans," he wrote, "and when the basement is dug and the foundation is in, I'll come down for a week and we'll rough it in." I was well acquainted with my father's enthusiasm for getting things done. But I was less than confident he could deliver on his prediction to take merely a week to "rough it in."

On the first Saturday of the project, the men assembled in their bib overalls and straw hats. By no means were they a paid construction force. These were church members and neighbors who came together every weekend to work on the parsonage because they felt they needed to get the job done, much like the men who felled the trees and showed up at the sawmill. They weren't afraid of hard work and knew how to shovel sand, gravel, and cement into a mixer. To my surprise, after a few weekends, we were ready for my father to make good on his promise.

Within hours after Dad's arrival, floor joists were in place, and we were raising studding for exterior and interior walls. For the first time in my life, I witnessed my dad's ability to direct people. He excelled at it. This was what he did in the aircraft industry. He wasn't going to do everything he promised in one week all by himself; he was going to accomplish it as part of a team. Before long, the house was roughed in; and it checked out precisely as the plans had dictated.

Can I help?

Putting partitions in place was just the beginning. Skilled craftsmen—electricians, plumbers, brick layers, heating installers, and others—were needed to finish the job.

A few men in the congregation who possessed those skills commuted to Roanoke or nearby towns every day to ply their trade. Their story brings a fascinating twist to the dream that started with a promise and finished with a house for the pastor.

During breaks in their normal workdays, these men sat together with their lunch buckets open, talking about their weekend activities, as most friends do. They discussed sports, upcoming family outings, hunting excursions, and what have you.

When the men from Goodview began talking about their weekend project, they told how they were building a parsonage for the church. Soon, a few of their work buddies asked if they could help. Suddenly, building the parsonage in Goodview became a major topic of conversation in nearby communities; and before we knew it, construction changed from a local venture to an areawide enterprise. We had complete crews with skills we never dreamed of. Things were getting done—and fast. At the end of two months, we had a beautiful parsonage.

Before the last brick was laid, the ladies of the Social Committee were planning the presentation ceremony. This was an historic achievement in the life of Goodview Baptist Church, and it deserved to be observed properly. Maxine insisted that the opening be kept simple. She knew and appreciated how much prayer, time, and effort went into building her new home; and she wanted a time for members of the church and community to walk through the house and see the place they worked so hard to make a reality.

After Clovis handed us the parsonage keys, I walked inside behind my wife. This would be her domain, and I wanted her to be the first to survey it for the two of us. For more than a year, we walked down a hill to the "facility" at the edge of the creek. Today we had two wonderful bathrooms, one upstairs and one downstairs; three beautiful bedrooms; a fully equipped kitchen; a dining room; a spacious living room; and a side porch far from the dust-belching road. A lovely, modern parsonage now stood proudly near Goodview Baptist Church. It was a spectacular accomplishment.

The congregation had delivered. The building looked better to us than the Taj Mahal. And what made it even more special was the knowledge that it had been built by our friends with love. "Can you believe this?" I asked, looking around.

"I can," Maxine replied quietly. "And you just wait and see what I'll be able to do with it." Maxine excelled at making do with almost nothing. I couldn't wait to see what she could do with something. "My first job," she said, "will be to get the guest room ready for the evangelist. Have you forgotten? Our revival is just around the corner."

There was no doubt where the evangelist would stay.

He'd be a guest of Goodview Baptist Church at the new parsonage. Everyone had come together on the project, much like the Israelites who rebuilt the walls of Jerusalem under the leadership of Nehemiah. They put their hands to the work and didn't stop until they finished. What God had started, He completed. And we were profoundly grateful.

Clockwise, top left: Elwood; Maxine;
Elwood and Maxine; Maxine's mother,
Florena (left), and Florena's sister Nora.

Clockwise, top left: steam engine, Peaks of Otter,
Homecoming, the van bringing children to Sunday
school, the Bedford Boys in Europe, train station.

Goodview Baptist Church in the 1950s

A New Parsonage for Goodview

Thomas Jefferson's Outhouse at Poplar Forest

Doctor Sam's Office

CHAPTER ELEVEN

I Think I Will

In rural communities like Goodview in the 1930s, '40s, and even the 1950s, recreation took preparation. Often it involved a long, dusty ride to a bowling alley, theater, or restaurant. The Post Office closed at 5. The depot locked up even earlier. Action at the Johnsons' store crept to a crawl after sunset. So, when revival meetings began, the community went to church. And a major event on the church's annual calendar was the fall revival.

Because church was the only game in town, so to speak, good attendance didn't imply deep spirituality. I would be hard-pressed to assert that all those whose posteriors plonked down on the sturdy, wooden pews came exclusively out of a deep hunger for God. That wasn't the case. It just turned out that church was where things were happening.

Revival speakers were either pastors from other areas or itinerant evangelists. In either case, they preached straightforward messages, never offering colorful homilies that disguised the gospel behind feel-good rhetoric. Revival meetings did not proffer salvation by osmosis. These men told you the plain truth straight out—that you were a lowdown sinner. And if you didn't get right with God and ask Him to save your sorry self through faith in the blood of Jesus Christ, you'd spend an eternity in torment wishing you had. If you didn't get the point, you were missing the message.

That's what the gospel is all about: God loves us so much He sent His only begotten Son to take the punishment we deserve. When we repent of our sin and place our faith in Jesus, He gives us forgiveness and everlasting life. Then we spend the rest of our lives loving Him and serving Him. Plain and simple.

Both the saint and the unconverted sinner alike knew exactly what was on tap for the evening revival. Most meetings had three distinct objectives:

(1) *Renewal.* The messages gave true believers in Jesus a concentrated opportunity to become spiritually warmed and revived by hearing the gospel that had revolutionized their lives. It was said that the preaching of the gospel saved Goodview, and many saints testified to that fact when they assembled to hear the message, to be refreshed in the Word, and to draw closer to their Lord.

(2) *Reclamation.* As was true in the days of the early church, some people were backslidden and needed to be restored. They had been damaged by grief, deception, dissention, or allurements; and the revival called them to repent and return to fellowship with their Savior and His people. In a sense, revival week at Goodview Baptist Church called all prodigals to return to the fold.

(3) *Redemption.* In those days, the call to come to Christ was not couched in comforting phraseology. The unconverted were *sinners* and sinners were *lost,* in need of being *saved.*

I Think I Will

During the Great Awakening in America (1730–1755), theologian Jonathan Edwards preached his famous sermon, "Sinners in the Hands of an Angry God." It got right to the point—so much so that some parishioners reportedly stood up and called out, "What shall I do to be saved?"

Their words echoed those of the Philippian jailer in the apostle Paul's day. He fell trembling before Paul and Silas and asked, "Sirs, what must I do to be saved?" (Acts 29:30).

They told him, "Believe on the Lord Jesus Christ" (v. 31). Edwards' message was reprised somewhat by an early 1960s evangelist who called one of his sermons "Turn or Burn." While one may question the propriety of such a title, the issue remains the same. After all, it was Jesus Himself who declared, "The Son of Man has come to seek and to save that which was lost" (Lk. 19:10). He also said, "Unless you repent you will all likewise perish" (13:3). That's why we preach the gospel. And that's why the gospel was front and center when bearers of the Good News stepped into the Goodview pulpit.

Casting the Net

The evangelist we had that year came highly recommended. He apparently specialized in short sermons and long invitations. As a service came to an end, parishioners bowed their heads and closed their eyes, and the preacher asked for a show of hands from those who felt in need of prayer.

As the congregation sang an invitation hymn, usually *Just as I am* or *Almost Persuaded,* the evangelist invited those who raised their hands to walk forward for counseling or to make a public profession of faith.

An intriguing aspect of the revival meetings was how

they often drew people, at least for a night or two, who scrupulously avoided showing up for services on a regular Sunday. I always suspected some of them put in an appearance during the revival to placate their wives who pleaded with them to join the family for church. So they came, much like the Christmas and Easter attendees who skip church every Sunday but seek a bit of tranquility on holidays and show up once or twice each year.

Of course, other issues also played into revival attendance. On any given evening, we probably had a few men among the regulars who were suspected of being distillers of unlicensed beverages. Also warming the pews were some of their customers, whose idea of a well-invested Saturday night usually involved sitting in pickup trucks on deserted backwoods roads listening to hounds run foxes or raccoons up dark hollows.

We always wondered who might break ranks with the unbelieving and respond to the altar call. In a small community where everyone knew everyone, being there when a friend or neighbor chose repentance and new life in Christ was something worth experiencing.

Interestingly, the flintiest resistors to the gospel would not enter the church. Some lounged against their vehicle's fenders near the open windows to listen to the proceedings while waiting to pick up family or neighbors they had brought to the services. The parking lot crowd increased perceptibly whenever the delegation from the Green Spring congregation was coming to sing.

We never knew who in the parking lot crowd might get saved. God had a way of surprising us. After all, the gospel is still the gospel, whether you hear it in a building or in a parking lot. It's still "the power of God to salvation for everyone who believes, for the Jew first and also for the Greek [Gentile]" (Rom. 1:16). Even guys sitting in their pickup trucks drinking bootleg whiskey from mason jars couldn't deny the transforming power of the gospel when God got hold of them.

Acie, Jubal, and Tom

The first few revival sessions drew only a paltry few during the altar calls, and the evangelist was not a happy man. "We've got to have a break in this meeting," he said emphatically.

Inexperienced as I was, I didn't know what he meant by *break* or how said break could be created. Maxine and I talked about it privately and concluded the best we could do was pray that the Lord would answer the need.

At the next meeting the following evening, while we sang the last stanza of *Just as I Am,* Acie—an affable man numbered among the fraternity of pickup-truck-sitting, midnight fox hunters—stepped into the aisle, took my hand, and said, "Preacher, I want to be saved."

Looking past Acie, I could see his godly wife, Sarah, her face in her hands, weeping profusely. When the invitation ended and Sarah had composed herself, she came to me. "Pastor," she said, "I've prayed for this to happen for thirty-five years. I'd almost given up, but now this."

That was all she could manage for the moment. It was the break the evangelist had been looking for. The next morning, Acie's profession of faith was the talk of the town. Everyone who visited Johnson's grocery or the Post Office heard the news and wanted to offer an opinion about what had taken place.

The evangelist was invigorated. "Let's make a visit to the fellow who owns the sawmill you told me about," he said. I had told him earlier how the community responded to the parsonage project, including some details about how out of character it seemed for Jubal Yancey to offer his services without a fee.

Frankly, I didn't hold out much hope that visiting Jubal would change anything. I didn't envision Jubal accepting Christ as His Savior. But at least we would show him we were interested in his spiritual well being.

When we arrived at the house, we found him alone. His wife, Caroline, was at work in Roanoke; and the girls were in school. After a few minutes of small talk, the evangelist got down to the matter at hand. On confirming that Jubal was not saved, he launched into the plan of salvation and pressed our host to settle things with the Lord right then and there.

"Not today," came the terse reply.

Undeterred, the evangelist took a verbal step back, repeated the plan of salvation, and posed the question again. "Not today," Jubal replied.

I would be hard pressed to calculate the number of times this exchange reoccurred that afternoon. As a proponent of maintaining friendly relations with people, believers or otherwise, I began to run short of patience with the guest speaker's high-pressured tactics. But as I wished for a quick getaway, I heard Jubal say, "I think I will." Jubal's words gave credibility to the salesmen's credo that one hundred noes don't count. You just want one yes.

On the drive back to the parsonage for lunch, the

evangelist raved about what this decision would bring to the revival. I was skeptical, an opinion I quickly shared with Maxine as soon as I was out of earshot of our speaker. To my way of thinking, the "decision" smacked more of exhaustion than enthusiasm.

I was wrong. That night, as people filed in for the service, Jubal Yancey, hat in hand, followed his beaming wife through the door of the church and into a pew.

The next day, while the evangelist was in Roanoke for a haircut, I decided to call on our local blacksmith, Tom Smith. A man given to strong drink, Tom had become so impaired the people of Goodview called him their resident alcoholic. It had been months since our last conversation when Tom told me straight out that he wanted to change his life for the better. In response, I told him about God's love for him, shared the gospel, and told him he could have the life-altering change he needed right then.

"I can't do it now," Tom replied, "I'm not good enough."

My words fell on deaf ears when I tried to explain that salvation is not about our good works or about our trying to become better people. Salvation is about what Christ did for us in our helplessness. Tom wasn't ready. So I left him as I had found him. *Would today be any different?* I wondered.

"Let me ask you a question, Tom," I said. "Are you any better now than the last time we talked?"

"No preacher. I'm worse."

That day, I knew Tom was almost there. He finally admitted He needed a Savior and was ready to rectify a mistake a lot of us make. He thought he had to make himself good enough to deserve salvation. None of us deserves salvation. We're all sinners. God doesn't ask us to clean ourselves up before we come to Him. He asks us to come to Him so that He can clean us up. Perhaps for the first time, Tom understood his spiritual condition, and he found salvation that day in Jesus Christ.

Jubal and Tom weren't the only ones God was changing. He was changing me, as well. I began to understand more about the depth of the sufficiency of faith. Our salvation does not depend on the means or methods used by God's messengers. At times, people come to Christ almost despite their tactics. It is the God-given gospel that utterly transforms a life and a lifestyle. That fact was clear based on what took place in Goodview that year.

Acie, Jubal, and Tom all demonstrated the reality of what God can do through His simple gift of grace. When the revival ended, hardly a Sunday passed without all three men showing up for church and sitting attentively on those old, wooden pews. Their faithful attendance by no means contributed to their redemption. It was the other way around: Their attendance gave evidence of it.

As I rejoiced over these men coming to faith, I had no idea that our next visitation would be disastrous.

I Think I Will

CHAPTER TWELVE

Who Was That Masked Man?

Like most rural towns, Goodview had its fair share of eccentrics. Among those was Cletus Norman.

Cletus's unbridled, outspoken devotion to the Lone Ranger and his native American companion, Tonto, made you question Cletus's perception of reality. So fervent was his passion that he told folks if they could only persuade the Lone Ranger to make the trip to Virginia, the people of Goodview could rid themselves of raucous troublemakers once and for all.

Some people swore Cletus actually believed the television heroes were real. Whether he did or not, he never budged from his fierce commitment to the prowess of the masked man and Tonto.

When my friend Jimmie Jones first told me about Cletus and his Lone Ranger addiction, I could almost (but not quite) relate. I, too, had been an attentive follower of the fictional Texas Ranger who chased outlaws and relentlessly purged evil from the Wild West. My association with the masked man and Tonto began at the Romulus Civic Theater

Saturday matinee, where I sat mesmerized with my grammar school friends as we watched the fictional hero battle the bad guys in a film filled with action and suspense. The adventures of the Lone Ranger kept us on the edge of our seats.

It was the mid 1930s, and the country was still struggling through the ravages of the Great Depression. Entertainment, except for radio, was hard to find. Kids my age gravitated to the world of pretend—where cowboy good guys always triumphed, and imagination transformed school playgrounds into sprawling vistas of the Old West.

I financed my Civic Theater excursions mainly with bottles. Merchants gave me two cents for every empty I returned. Six garnered twelve cents, which covered ten cents for a movie ticket and two cents for candy. That worked for me!

Culture didn't sit high on my list at the Civic. Fred Astaire whirling Ginger Rogers across a ballroom floor did nothing to keep a boy looking for action focused on the screen. My friends and I winced at the Hollywood sophisticates as we poked one another in the ribs, snickering and laughing. Before we knew it, Art the ticket taker was rushing up and down the aisles shushing us and threatening us with expulsion if we didn't keep quiet.

Action-packed thrillers were our style. We sat spellbound by the planet-hopping exploits of Flash Gordon; the whip-snapping crusades of the caped vigilante, Zorro; the swashbuckling adventures of Buck Rogers; and the airborne escapades of Tailspin Tommy. These were our stock-in-trade.

But of all the heroes who sprung to life on the screen at the Civic, the Lone Ranger topped them all. Who can forget how he Hi-Yo-Silvered away after disposing of some wretched villain? Most episodes closed with the grateful recipients of deliverance gazing into the hills as the Ranger rode away and asking, "Who was that masked man?" Those immortal words sent us to our homes intrigued by the desire to learn more about the man behind the mask as we anticipated the following week's adventure.

As I listened to Jimmie explain Cletus Norman's fixation with the Lone Ranger, I was amused to think that, after all these years, Lone Ranger lore so vividly lived on in my own memory. Though I didn't exactly see myself as Cletus's kindred spirit, I at least had a clue where he was coming from.

However, when Maxine told me the Norman family had invited the evangelist and me to dinner, I was surprised. Cletus and his wife, Rachel, did not attend our church, though their children were regulars at Sunday school. I later learned their teen-aged daughter had begged her parents to invite us.

Silver or Trigger?

Before we left for the Norman house, I thought it best to fill the evangelist in on Cletus's Lone Ranger attachment, as Jimmie had explained it to me. I made sure to tell him not to bring it into the conversation.

Cletus had five children. Among them were two young teens whom I feared would be embarrassed if their father launched into his theories on what the Lone Ranger and Tonto could do if we called on them to rid Goodview of miscreants.

When we arrived, we were ushered into the living room to

wait for Cletus's wife, Rachel, to finish her dinner preparations and seat us in the dining room. The second I entered the living room, I felt like I had stepped into a different world. It was a shrine to the Lone Ranger. Memorabilia hung from every wall. Cletus, however, did not mention his idol or anything on display, talking instead about his work crafting furniture at the factory in Roanoke.

When Rachel called us into the dining room, I breathed a sigh of relief. We had avoided the dreaded subject and could now confine our comments to the delicious fried chicken, mashed potatoes, and garden-fresh green beans that lay before us. Then the honored guest posed a question, and my euphoria evaporated. "Cletus, if you could have any horse in the West, which one would you choose?"

Suddenly, I lost my appetite. The man at the head of the table also lost his, but for an entirely different reason. He was ready to rise to the occasion. "That's a hard one," he said after a brief pause.

"Now you take Trigger," said Cletus. "He'd be tough to beat. When Roy asked him to, I've even seen him kneel down and pray. I don't know that a horse anywhere in the world has ever done that before."

Trigger was the magnificent palomino stallion of Roy Rogers, a man who vied for the top spot on the king-of-the-cowboys roster long dominated by the famed Gene Autry and Hopalong Cassidy. Both of those men had achieved superstar status. Although Rogers would one day surpass them both, his rising popularity would not budge men who held loyalties to someone else. Cletus Norman was a case in point.

After a moment to reflect on the preacher's question,

Cletus made his decision. "Silver has done things I've never even seen Trigger do. One time the Lone Ranger and Tonto were tied up by some men who were on their way to rob a bank. But the Lone Ranger whistled for Silver, and that horse came over and untied them with his teeth. So I think I'm going to have to go with Silver."

Unfortunately, that answer did not end the conversation. Cletus was delighted the preacher wanted to know more and happily filled him in on the Lone Ranger's prowess in ridding the West of criminals. During what was left of the evening, the conversation continued to spiral downward. Finally, I reminded the evangelist that the evening service would soon be upon us, and we needed to get back. So we expressed our appreciation for the Normans' hospitality and left.

Bad Manners and a Lesson Learned

After our departure, the preacher was in a jovial mood. I was not. What I had just witnessed disturbed me.

A man who certainly should have known better had entertained himself at the expense of someone unaware that he was being mocked. And he did it in front of the man's wife and children, who knew exactly what was happening. Cletus Norman was a hard-working husband, father, and good citizen. Sure, he held fast to a harmless fantasy that others had long since abandoned. But exploiting Cletus's weakness and humiliating him for a few moments of personal amusement seemed to me a heartless thing to do.

The experience left a bitter taste in my mouth. Unfortunately, it exhibited a fact of life in ministry that I had not previously considered. Even though our visiting evangelist came to us "highly recommended," he still belonged to the human race, through which runs a common thread: sin. No matter how gifted a person may be in ministry, he still possesses human frailties common to us all. No one is sinless, and no one is perfect. If you put someone on a pedestal, he'll no doubt disappoint you, given enough time.

That is probably one reason the book of Hebrews tells us to keep our eyes focused on Jesus, "the author and finisher of our faith" (Heb. 12:2). It doesn't matter how old or young or rich or poor or humble or proud or educated or ignorant someone is. We are still all sinners, even those of us who are saved by grace.

God, on the other hand, will never disappoint. So it's best to keep our eyes on Him.

CHAPTER THIRTEEN

A Bad Day at the Outhouse

Jimmie Jones was on the other end of the phone. A catastrophe had just struck at his father's house, but Jimmie wouldn't tell me the details because he thought his father, Tut Jones, Goodview's postmaster, was better equipped to fill me in.

The Tut Jones residence was located in a type of rural suburb, up the hill and across the railroad tracks from what passed as the village's commercial center. Historically, Tut's family played a prominent role in Goodview life for longer than most folks could remember.

One celebrated piece of Goodview folklore involved Tut's father, Solomon Jones, a Civil War veteran who chose incarceration rather than sign a parole and pledge of loyalty to the United States government when the war ended in 1865. As a soldier in the Army of Northern Virginia, Solomon was among the remnants of General Robert E. Lee's tattered forces that surrendered to Union General Ulysses S. Grant at Appomattox, a few miles from his home in Goodview.

While most of Lee's men willingly signed the parole, took the pledge, and headed for home, Solomon steadfastly refused. To his way of thinking, it was one thing to lose in battle but quite another to promise to embrace flag and foe by rejoining the Union. So, Solomon stayed in jail.

As with all legendary accounts, the story got better and better with each retelling, and people speculated on how long the dissenter held out before finally returning to the comforts of home.

When Maxine and I arrived in the hamlet, Solomon's son Tut was the postmaster and a prominent face in the community, as well as in our church. Tut's brother, Grady, a confirmed bachelor, lived alone at the old homestead but spent a considerable amount of time with Tut and Tut's wife, Lee, either at their dinner table or snoozing on their veranda on warm summer afternoons.

Jimmie knew what he was doing when he left it to his father to give me the full story of what had taken place. No one could spin a yarn like Tut Jones. Tut possessed descriptive abilities capable of bringing every detail to life, along with a rare talent for lacing his observations with wry splashes of humor. He was like a rural version of Art Buchwald, the Pulitzer Prize-winning humorist whose newspaper columns had people laughing across America.

And there was no doubt that what happened that day at the Jones house—actually, the Jones outhouse—was worthy of Buchwaldian flair.

A Forgotten Institution

When Englishman Thomas Crapper pulled the chain on one of the first privies capable of operating inside a domicile, history was being made. Although many people falsely credit him with inventing the toilet, Mr. Crapper did own a plumbing company and improved the water closet by inventing the floating ballcock.

Remarkably, hardly a whiff of history endures that describes how radically indoor plumbing changed the face of much of the Western world. When I was young, you could find a row of outhouses lining alleys, serving residents of the homes in front. Each edifice reflected the resident's taste in architectural design and artistic panache, revealing a good bit about those who frequented the facility.

Here in Virginia, a compelling feature of Founding Father Thomas Jefferson's mansions (Monticello in Charlottesville and his getaway, Poplar Forest, near Lynchburg) are the impeccably designed, octagonal-shaped brick privies standing discreetly behind greenery that obscures the view from the main quarters. Interestingly, tourists today seem as keen on visiting the outhouses as they are the main residences.

And why not? Outhouses are part of Americana. They boasted a variety of shapes and sizes. There were one-holers, two-holers, and three-holers. Three-holers were top of the line, not only because they accommodated three people at a time (usually a parent and children) but because they had a larger storage capacity for waste.

Waste could be a problem. An outhouse's hole in the ground usually filled up within a year, making it necessary to dig a new hole and move the structure to a new resting place. Determining exactly how far to move it and where to dig the new hole was almost an art form, considering the consequences of miscalculation.

Although Tut Jones's comfort facility lacked Thomas Jefferson's aesthetic embellishments, it served the purpose of its calling, providing functionality through simplicity. The small building sported a crescent-shaped opening neatly cut into the door, a whitewashed interior, and an outdated stack of *Roanoke Times* newspapers, along with a cast-off Sears & Roebuck catalog. A screen door latched on the inside for privacy.

As millions of all-weather comfort stations passed into disuse with the advent of indoor plumbing, the men who specialized in outhouse relocation found themselves out of work. Goodview, being a small, off-the map sort of place, still had a significant number of specialists who skillfully tackled projects others hesitated to undertake. When it was time to relocate the Jones outhouse, Buck Daniels was your man.

Buck was a true professional in the art of outhouse excavation and relocation—a sort of outhouse engineer. This was a fellow who brooked no nonsense when it came to his chosen profession. Thin as a whippet and deceptively strong, Buck prided himself on his punctiliousness and precision. In every respect, he was the guy for the job. Being a man of few words, Buck preferred to ply his craft alone, never fouling his day with benign conversation.

So, it was no surprise that it was Buck Daniels who stood beside Postmaster Jones early that warm July morning, laying out his vision for relocating the Jones family outhouse. After Buck paced off a distance from the current site to the proposed location, he explained that moving the privy forward a bit more would save everyone a few steps getting there and avoid the need to cut a new path to the entrance—an arrangement that seemed appropriate to Mr. Jones.

After authorizing Buck's proposal, Tut headed off to the

Post Office, leaving word that he would return at lunch to check on the work.

"As soon as I got home for lunch," Tut told me, "I went out back to check on Buck. He was down on his knees, squaring out the corners of the pit with a small trowel."

"I'll have this done here pretty soon," Buck called up from the hole.

"'Well, as soon as you're finished, come up to the house. Lee's fixing lunch for us,' I told him. As I was turning to leave, I saw what looked like a bulge beginning to form on the opposite side of the wall from where Buck was working. Before I could say anything, the whole wall collapsed, burying Buck in a landslide of dirt and stuff from the hole being replaced.

"For a minute, I thought we'd lost him, Pastor. But then he stood up and headed for the ladder."

Buck had miscalculated and inadvertently punctured the wall keeping better than a year's worth of waste in check. It wasn't in check any longer. It was all over Buck. "Was he alright?" I asked.

"I didn't know at first," Tut said. "He just stood there, covered in muck, looking back into the hole. Then he spoke. 'Do you want me to go back in after the mattock and shovel?' he asked me.

"'No Buck,' I said. 'I think we'll just write this off as a construction loss.'"

Determining what to do next would have to wait until after lunch. Like many other wives, Miss Lee (everyone called Tut's wife "Miss Lee") was a stickler for serving food when it was still hot. Grady, Tut's brother, had already arrived, so things in the kitchen were in order. However, elsewhere they were anything but ready.

Tut and Grady had taken Buck out back to the wash house, where they pumped water up from the well and filled a tub for Buck so he could wash off the stink. Meanwhile, Lee threw a cloth over the table in a vain attempt to keep her food warm. Then she rummaged through her husband's dresser, pulling out some old clothes for Buck to change into after his bath.

As it happened, Buck stood over six feet tall. Tut was almost a foot shorter. So, Buck emerged looking like everything he had on shrunk in a laundry apocalypse. With the pants riding halfway to his knees and the shirt sleeves coming halfway to his elbows, he looked like a refugee from a comic strip. But Buck didn't seem to mind, and everything was appropriately covered in time to get to the business of eating.

For the most part, the cleanup had put the outhouse engineer into presentable condition, or so everyone thought until the four were well into their lunch. Suddenly, Grady shoved his chair back and ordered, "Open that door, Lee! I've had about all I can take!"

It turns out the outhouse aroma snuck into the house anyway by way of Buck's shoes. Despite all Mrs. Jones did to replace Buck's clothing with her husband's, she couldn't come close to finding anything in Buck's shoe size.

The fiasco got me thinking about how the Lord must view us. In our human frailty, we see ourselves as cleaned up and smelling pretty good. Or at least we try hard to clean ourselves up. But no matter what we do, God still smells the stink. We can't remove it. It's the stink of sin that permeates our souls, and only Jesus Christ can remove it when we repent and ask Him for forgiveness.

After He saves us, we diffuse "the fragrance of His knowledge in every place" and "are to God the fragrance of Christ among those who are being saved and among those who are perishing" (2 Cor. 2:14–15). God makes us new creations in Him, and we become a sweet-smelling aroma to Him. Much better than stinking like an outhouse.

Opportunity Out of Calamity

It turns out the collapse of the privy wall worked in Lee Jones's favor. Miss Lee was a delightful person to be around. In addition to being a magnificent cook, she exhibited flawlessly the qualities of gracious hospitality as commended in Scripture. One of her most endearing features was her ability to laugh at herself and retain a sense of excitement about life.

For example, she had a problem with her eyesight and once mistook a bottle of liniment for a bottle of vanilla. She poured a healthy dose into the hand-cranked ice cream maker, and when her watery-eyed guests discovered the mistake, Miss Lee had a quick appraisal. "I guess we've made history here tonight," she said. "You are the first people in the world to have tasted Lee Jones Horse Liniment Vanilla Ice Cream!"

Lee also could drive when most women didn't know how. It was an occasion when Tut and Miss Lee passed by in their ancient green Chevy on their way to Roanoke to go shopping. Tut sat bolt upright in the seat beside his wife, offering unappreciated commentary on her chauffeuring skills, while Lee held a death grip on the steering wheel as she maneuvered her way over the bumpy dirt roads.

But this day's events evoked a different demeanor from the lady of the house. She set aside her normally cheery disposition and sat her husband down for a serious conversation about plumbing.

"I hope you learned something today," she began. "I've been telling you for a long time that we should have an inside bathroom. We're not getting any younger, and heaven knows it's time to do something about it."

Heaven most certainly did know. It was Tut who needed to be reminded. "If we're going to do it, it should be done this summer while we have decent weather," she said. "And it won't be any trouble to walk a few more steps to use Jimmie's toilet while it's being put in."

No one was around to ascertain whether it was Miss Lee's powers of persuasion or the day's catastrophic outhouse collapse that induced Tut's swift surrender. But he replied, "I'll call Randall [a builder] in the morning and ask him to come over and see what he can do."

In the end, tragedy turned to triumph. Miss Lee would have her bathroom, Buck would have his job (only this time he would be digging horizontal trenches for sewer lines, rather than vertical holes in the ground), and Mr. Jones could plan his work at the Post Office in peace.

Not such a bad day after all.

CHAPTER FOURTEEN

In Pursuit of Houdini

Harry Houdini, the Hungarian-born son of a rabbi, made Americans hold their breath for nearly three decades through a torrent of spectacular escapes from death-defying situations. Houdini performed in the 1920s, when the mood of the era was "Let the good times roll." Flappers, speakeasies, and entrepreneurs of thrill were enjoying their heydays before the Great Depression turned the corner and slapped them all down.

In the meantime, the rabbi's son enthralled the masses. His forte was escape. He could escape from anything. Handcuffed and stuffed into water-filled milk cans, shackled and hung upside down in the notorious "Chinese Water Torture Cell," buried alive—Houdini escaped them all. The "King of Handcuffs" reigned supreme.

Goodview's Houdini

Although no record exists of the master illusionist ever setting foot anywhere near Goodview, the hamlet did have someone it could lay claim to: Buck Daniels. Buck's mastery in the art of escape probably surpassed his prowess in outhouse engineering. He was unrivaled when it came to avoiding pastors and evangelists interested in his spiritual welfare.

Buck lived with two spinster sisters, Martha and Samantha, in a comfortable farmhouse on the outskirts of the village. Most evenings, the sisters could be found sitting together on the airy, screened-in front porch sipping tall, cool glasses of homemade iced tea. When not otherwise engaged, Buck would keep them company. Though conversation was sparse, the tea was all you really needed to enjoy a relaxing sit-down before retiring for the night.

The sisters, both former teachers, comported themselves with dignity and refinement, earning them a high degree of respect from everyone throughout the community. Unfortunately, younger brother Buck did not share Martha and Samantha's standards of conduct. Not that he could be called the black sheep of the family. Buck simply chose his own path. His disinterest in church and God greatly worried his sisters, who often expressed their concern to me, accompanied by an appeal to talk to Buck about his need for the Lord in his life. If he got saved, they would be enormously relieved.

On the Lookout for the Preacher

It was common knowledge that the standard Baptist night for church visitation was Thursday. At any time during respectable hours, the pastor and whoever happened to be with him that evening could knock on your door and expect to be let in to discuss spiritual matters.

In my case, it was Jim Thomason who almost always

accompanied me on visitation. No one regarded as intrusive or inconvenient this random method of calling on people. In today's culture, everyone makes appointments for almost everything. But Thursday night visitation predated that practice. When folks wanted to see someone, they just dropped by.

True, sometimes it could be a problem. The Thursday night drop-by became predictable. So, on Thursday evenings, Buck made himself scarce. Unwilling to take a chance that Jim and I might come looking for him, he never joined his sisters on the porch.

One night after I returned home from the Danielses' farmhouse and expressed my disappointment at having missed Buck yet again, Maxine asked if she could offer a suggestion. "If you really want to catch up with him, I can tell you how to do it."

"Yeah? What do you know that I don't?" I asked.

"It's simple. Just go on another night. Make it Tuesday instead of Thursday."

Why hadn't I thought of that? Her comeback exposing the obvious jolted me. I had become locked into convention. Why not Tuesday? "I'll call Jim!" I replied.

When Jim and I pulled into the Danielses' driveway the following Tuesday at teatime, there was Buck. Trapped, like a rat in a cage. There was nowhere for him to go except to the door to invite us in.

"Just a minute," he said politely. "I'll get chairs for you."

As we sat down, Martha got up and started for the kitchen to bring us tea. "Don't bother," Buck told her. "I'll get it while I'm up."

Martha, Samantha, Jim, and I chatted for a few minutes

as we waited for the tea. After awhile, Martha stood up and headed toward the kitchen, explaining that Buck was probably brewing a fresh pot.

Too late. Just before she left, I heard a screen door close somewhere at the back of the house. Houdini had pulled off another escape. In the six years I ministered in Goodview, I never was able to sit down with Buck for a serious conversation about his need of Christ. He always managed to get away, which saddened me and left me with a lingering sense of disappointment.

Many years later, long after his sisters were gone, I received word that Buck had become a believer. I was overjoyed. His story reminded me that saving people is God's job. Only He can save a soul. He tells us, "Always be ready to give a defense to everyone who asks you for the hope that is in you" (1 Pet. 3:15). It's our responsibility to present the gospel, but it's God's job to do the rest. And when His time is right, we can rest assured He will always have someone in place to show people the way home.

Miracle on Brushy Creek Road

Newcomers moving into Goodview were a rarity. Therefore, when a new family showed up, news traveled fast; and finding information about them became a high priority.

One day we got word the Scruggses had arrived from the Pearisburg area in northern Virginia and that Mr. Scruggs worked for a power company based in Roanoke. I planned to call on the family as soon as possible with an offer of assistance and an invitation to join us on Sunday at church. Ladies from the congregation were never far behind with plates of food, vegetables, cakes, pies, and offers to help the newcomers get settled.

Brushy Creek Road lay across the creek from the village's main residential area. Not being familiar with all the roads, I was always glad to have Jim with me when I visited people. Jim Thomason knew the territory and saved me much time looking for places.

Jim was a great companion, not only on our visitation expeditions but in a million other ways as well. After he installed water in the old parsonage kitchen, we became good friends. Jim was all about serving God and being available to anyone in need. He possessed an uninhibited commitment to do the right thing without expectation of reward or applause.

As a boy, the only stable influence in his life was his godly mother. One of his earliest memories was getting down on his knees beside her as she prayed for him. Unfortunately, she died when he was very young. Orphaned, he was sent to live with ne'er-do-well relatives who were lazy, irresponsible, and lived as contradictions to everything his mother had prayed for him.

Consequently, Jim approached manhood uneducated, without direction in his life, and beset by an unrelenting emptiness. He was not a rabblerouser or troublemaker, like many around him. He was simply a soul adrift.

Then one Sunday morning, to everyone's surprise, Jim walked into church alone and without previous invitation. When the altar call was given, he stepped into the aisle and walked forward. When the pastor asked him why he had done so, Jim replied, "I want to be saved."

During one of our talks, I asked him how he had concluded that he wanted to give his life to Christ. "Because,"

Jim said, "it just came to a time when I wanted to find what my mother had." His mother was long gone, but her prayers still lingered.

In the book of Revelation, twenty-four elders fall down before the Lamb of God. Each elder holds "a harp, and golden bowls full of incense, which are the prayers of the saints" (5:8). Our prayers are precious to the Lord. He loves when we pray. Jim's mother's prayers no doubt ascended to heaven like sweet-smelling incense; and when the time was right, God reached down and saved her son.

From that life-transforming day, Jim Thomason became an unassuming, devoted, no-nonsense follower of Jesus Christ. And I was glad he was with me to visit the Scruggses.

"I think that's the place we're looking for," I told him as we drove by a home on the left.

"No preacher," Jim replied. "I believe it's the one we just passed."

"Going by what Eldon told me in his directions," I said, "it's this one. Let's try it."

A matronly lady came to the door. "If you're looking for the Scruggs house, it's just back up the road."

Not a word from Jim, nor an apology from me. We just turned around and headed back. We pulled into another driveway and walked up to the house. Answering my knock on the door was a young woman I supposed to be in her early 20s. Before I even could introduce us, she asked, "Are you a preacher, mister?"

"Why, yes I am," I replied.

"Could you come in and explain to me and my brother how to be saved?"

It's a rare occasion to pull up to the home of a total

stranger who immediately asks about salvation. "Yes, of course we can, and we will," I said. "But before we do, may I ask you how you've come to ask the question?"

Her answer astonished me. "Well, we have been listening to a preacher on the radio. He kept saying that we need to be saved. But he didn't tell us how to be saved. So, after the program, we prayed; and I asked God to send someone to tell us how to get to heaven."

And there we were! Knocking on her door! An answer to her prayer.

We sat down before an open Bible and explained the way of salvation. We gave her the gospel and answered her questions and those of her teen-aged brother. Obviously, God had prepared their hearts, and they were ready to receive His gift of everlasting life. Jim and I counted it a privilege to be there when it all came together.

"Jim," I said as we drove away, "we've witnessed a miracle tonight." We both knew that any time someone experiences the new birth, it's a miracle. But for the two of us, this appointment was a once-in-a-lifetime experience. Never again would I see redemption transacted in such a dramatic fashion.

God has His way of doing things. And it's a genuine blessing when He chooses to use us. Someone else led Buck Daniels to Christ. Jim and I were used to lead these young people. "Unless the LORD builds the house, they labor in vain who build it" (Ps. 127:1). The Builder knows which of His workers He wants for each house. We were sure glad that day He chose us.

Florena Fiscus Zollars

CHAPTER FIFTEEN

Mom

Summer had arrived, and with it came the week of our annual vacation, when we stuffed the trunk of the car and pulled off the dusty roads to head west. Our destination lay nearly six hundred miles away in Sumner, Illinois, the place where Maxine grew up and her mom waited for us. Mom, too, was packing because, after our few days with her there, she would join us to spend quality time with us in Goodview.

Our plan was to leave early Tuesday morning after tidying up a few details on Monday to avoid being tracked down hundreds of miles away because of some urgent situation I had left unattended. A major part of my Monday would be to visit a man in the community named Del Wheeler who was reported to be in serious condition.

Dell was well connected in the Goodview male establishment; and though partially paralyzed, he operated a thriving business that seemed to me an oddity because his enterprise was selling illegal liquor.

The Goodview Alcohol Beverage Commission

There's a saying in business that an indispensable element to success is location. Del Wheeler had an excellent location. His base of operations stood just off the main road into and out of the village, which made quick stops and getaways easy for customers not wishing to be spotted.

In addition to selling illegal liquor, Del was a skilled importer of the merchandise. Though handicapped, he had an unidentified "runner" who carried moonshine from sources in Franklin County, located across the Roanoke River from Goodview. Once called the Moonshine Capital of the World, Franklin County had been notorious for stills that produced unlicensed alcohol long before the Great Depression. In fact, the trade's longevity gave rise to palpable resentment of government interference in the clandestine distilling industry. As one resident put it, "I just don't see that the government has a right to regulate what a man does with his own corn."

It was alleged that, for the more discriminating, Del offered legal liquor purchased at state ABC outlets for resale at marked-up prices—a practice also illegal.

That was the business, which seemed at cross purposes with the character of the man I found during my visits. While Del was somewhat elusive about his commitment to personal faith, he talked effusively about theology, particularly when it came to prophetic passages of Scripture. He often retrieved his Bible from a nightstand while making a point.

Sometimes we talked so long I could see cars slowly driving by waiting for the preacher to leave so they could stop in and transact business. My host never seemed to care. He knew they would wait.

Fortunately, on this occasion, his condition was not as dire as reported. We had a nice chat, and I left reasonably assured that my vacation would not be interrupted by an urgent call informing us of the need to return to minster to Del's family and attend to funeral arrangements.

The Great Adventure

Our trip to Maxine's hometown took approximately ten hours. We had to be at the starting gate by 5 a.m. Aside from stops to refuel and refresh, the only major pull-off would be for lunch, usually in some shaded area on the side of the road. We'd eat cold fried chicken, potato salad, and drinks from the ice chest, all of which gave us sustenance to get on with the rest of the trip.

Sumner, Illinois, impressed me as a place famed author Samuel Clemens (Mark Twain) would have found comfortable for spinning more Tom Sawyer and Huckleberry Finn-like tales. The town was located in the southeastern part of the state across the Wabash River from Vincennes, Indiana. Christy Avenue, the main thoroughfare, looked like a place trying to make it into the twentieth century but never quite succeeding.

The street was excessively wide. A couple of hitching rails remained from the horse-and-buggy days, when the road needed to be wide to accommodate that mode of transportation.

For the most part, Sumner was a laid-back town where well-to-do farmers came to retire and spend their days on benches in front of the Sumner Savings and Loan, talking crops and weather. In addition to being the ideal place to get away and wind down from the stress of must-do living, Sumner was a great spot to grow a family. You could walk anywhere in a few minutes. The smooth cement sidewalks accommodated pedestrians and were perfect for kids on roller skates to spend warm afternoons expelling pent-up energy.

On many a sunny afternoon in the 1930s, you could find young Maxine cruising along the sidewalks on her roller skates, her long, dark hair blowing in the wind. I met her soon after she moved to Romulus to live with her married sister. We were in the ninth grade. Maxine was outside watching her brother-in-law repair a window. Suddenly, I saw this vision of rare beauty standing there. I immediately walked over, feigning interest in the window. But I couldn't take my eyes off Maxine. I stood there with my mouth open. That was it. There was never anyone for me after that but Maxine Zollars.

When we arrived in Sumner, we found Florena Fiscus Zollars sitting in a rocking chair on the porch of her house on Carey Street, waiting for us. Mom was diminutive in height—two inches below the five-foot mark. But the lack in physical dimension in no way diminished her stature as a mother or a candidate for the Greatest Generation hall of fame.

She was born in 1894 into a prominent family whose roots stemmed from the pioneer period, when land-hungry settlers chopped and sawed their way through virgin forests to find a new home on the frontier of expansionist America. Flo was the darling of her father, Oliver J. Fiscus, and his wife, Emma. She loved riding beside him on trips to town in their burnished buggy behind a splendid pair of matched horses. As she matured, she became one of the most sought-after prospects for marriage.

Sunday concerts in the park, where the Sumner volunteer band played John Philip Sousa marches and *Good Old Summertime* melodies, was the place to be. People loved spending the afternoon there, listening to music and socializing with friends. That was where Flo caught the eye of young Everett, who peered out at the crowd as he played the trumpet.

Their subsequent courtship consummated in marriage. Young Flo married for love, only to be betrayed by a philandering husband who would desert her and their six children. With both of her parents gone, she managed to sustain the family for a time by selling off trees from the land left to her as an inheritance. But with the Great Depression ravaging the economy, virtually everyone struggled to make it.

The logical course for Flo and her family seemed drastic but necessary. "We'll take the boys" (Robert, Lee, and Everett), said a sincerely solicitous uncle. "I can use them to help work the farm, and we're near the school."

Cousin Cathleen and her husband, Lewis, who were childless, offered to take Maxine. "It would be wonderful to have her as a daughter," they told Flo. The other girls, Violet and Dorothy, would remain with Florena because the town doctor had hired them to do housekeeping.

This was the solution proffered. Though partially separated, the family would still be intact, and Flo would see her children from time to time. Her answer was quick in coming. She thanked everyone for their kindness but would not give up her children. She was their mother, and she would raise them. When asked how, she replied, "I'll find a way to make ends meet." And she did. She made do.

Along with working mornings in the kitchen at a local eatery, she kept a large garden and chickens. And with some help from Franklin Roosevelt's Civilian Conservation Corps where her sons Lee and Rob served turns, Mom kept her family together. She made ends meet and kept her word.

During those difficult years, she proved she was never merely an ornament on her father's buggy. Flo's mothering skills involved more than putting food on the table. She instilled in her children a quality of character and desire for accomplishment.

At the onset of World War II, she saw her sons off to different branches of the armed services. Lee served in the Pacific, fighting on jungle-infested islands with the U.S. Army as it moved toward the Japanese mainland. Robert fought in North Africa, Sicily, and Italy against Hitler's Axis troops. Everett, the youngest, served in the navy.

Back on Carey Street, Flo passed the long nights wondering if she would end up hanging one or more gold star banners in her window, as others in town did when they lost their sons in some far-off war zone. She spent her days crocheting and knitting enough pillow covers, afghans, doilies, scarves, and assorted items to fill several closets as a distraction to keep from thinking about what might happen to her sons away at war.

Funds sent to her through the government from her sons or mother's aid agencies were walked to the bank to be deposited into accounts she intended to use to give each of the boys a good start when they returned from the service.

Selflessness was but one of the characteristics of this small woman of huge stature.

My wife's mother rarely dropped a word about herself. She preferred conversation about the children, relatives, or items of interest in the *Sumner Press*. Reading the local gossip was one excess she allowed herself. Investing a hard-earned dollar or so for an annual subscription gave her every snippet of information she needed about where folks had been, what they were up to, who had died, and what was going on in the town and in the church without setting a foot outside her door.

An inescapable obligation of every visit we made to Maxine's hometown was a trip to the cemetery with Mom. Perhaps it indicated the meager offerings available for entertainment in Sumner. But being an avid tombstone reader myself, it was an event I looked forward to.

Strolling through a rural cemetery is like taking a journey through local history. Every gravesite has a story. Even the small building used as a storage shed had a memorable past. It was there that bleachers were raised, a small platform erected, and band instruments readied for Sumnerites who would gather to commemorate national days of remembrance.

Maxine's mom told me she used to leap from the family buggy to join her friends on the fringes of standing-room-only crowds of townspeople dressed in their best finery. They had turned out to hear speeches from local dignitaries while the band played music that echoed across the fields filled with granite memorials. For Flo and her friends, the best part of the day came when ceremonies ended, and the crowd dispersed to pay their respects at family plots. That left the children free to enjoy playing together.

Over the years, I've learned that every cemetery or memorial garden seems to have at least one story steeped in mystery, reserved to be retold in hushed tones tinged with a sense of foreboding. In Sumner's acres of rest for the departed, the story involved an unmarked grave located near the woods lining one side of the cemetery. Buried there were the remains of a man who attempted to rob the town's bank and, for his effort, got shot and killed. He had no identification, and no one in town knew him. So he was buried in what passed as Sumner's potter's field.

But the drama did not end there. Apparently, several times a year, a bouquet of fresh flowers would appear on the grave. No one ever seemed to know who put it there. In a small town like Sumner, there were an abundance of suspects but never a conclusion concerning who might have known or, perhaps, even loved the man. In the end, he left behind both the money from his failed bank robbery and the tale of his misfortune, which has been retold for decades.

The days I spent in my mother-in-law's company on her turf enlightened and inspired me. On our walks through the cemetery, she introduced me to people of another century—people who had tasted hardship and deprivation the likes of which I had not known. Flo herself was among those people, and I admired her—men and women who worked hard and did what needed to be done without fanfare or expectations of gratitude. I guess you could say their unassuming determination to make ends meet defined their generation.

That quality of character transcends regions. I witnessed it in the weathered faces of the women in Goodview who wore poke bonnets, tended their gardens, provided for their families, and took in others to raise and care for when hardships struck.

That's why, when we brought Flo home with us to Virginia, she fit right in. It was her kind of place, and the people of Goodview were her kind of people.

Let's Pick Some Berries

As summer arrived, fences and embankments grew heavy with blackberries. After a few days of recuperating from our trip west to pick up my mother-in-law, our conversation turned to blackberry jam, blackberry cobblers, and other assorted blackberry delicacies.

This was the season when factories turning sand into glass containers made fortunes. Although moonshiners depended heavily on mason jars to store their products, the moonshine industry became but a small niche in the glass business when it was canning season in America.

In addition to everyone's enthusiasm for the delights of the seedy black fruit, we got the word from the berry experts, "They're really good for you, too." How good were they? Well, they were touted to slow the growth of cancers, improve brain function, reduce inflammation, help the heart, and promote healthy skin. So those who ventured into the brambles were, unbeknown to them, on a medical mission!

Growing up in Michigan, the berry of choice for our family was the raspberry, which actually turned out to be a minor player in the McQuaid canning arsenal. My mother was a connoisseur of canning foodstuffs; and Dad's large garden kept steam bubbling from pans on the kitchen stove for hours in the summer. Tomatoes, beans, pickles, and anything that could be committed to a mason jar was stuffed inside.

Near summer's end, when the threat of frost began to chill the evening air, we rushed to pick the green tomatoes still hanging on the vines. With a sprig of dill, a little vinegar, and pinch of garlic, the green goodness could be preserved throughout the winter. In addition, green tomatoes could be sliced, battered, and fried, creating the romance of the fried green tomato promoted by people who, in my opinion, had never eaten one. By summers' end, our shelves sagged from the weight of long rows of canned goods, assuring hearty meals for months to come.

What Mother Never Told Me

Before we made our foray into the woods on our Goodview berry-picking expedition, we assembled the glassware and jar lids essential to the canning of jams and jellies. They had to be ready for the pailfuls and baskets full of the succulent fruit we would bring home.

I, too, was ready. Pails and baskets hanging from my expectant arms, off I went into the woods in search of berries. Unbeknown to me, an army of chiggers lurked in the tall grass before the berry vines, awaiting my arrival. They hitched a ride on my legs and torso as I foraged for fruit. While I picked the berries, ignorance was bliss. I went about filling my pails, completely unaware of what would befall me by week's end.

On Saturday, one day before I had to preach, the full effects of chigger infestation descended. I was covered with red bumps, accompanied by intense itching. By Sunday morning, restraining the urge to scratch was nearly impossible.

When I entered the pulpit, I knew I had to keep my bug bites from becoming a major distraction. God was good. I pronounced the benediction, went home, and slathered herbal concoctions all over the chigger bites for the next few days until I recovered.

Was the reward—jams and jellies—worthy of the torment? I'm still trying to figure that one out.

Flashlight and Crackers

As summer receded and color began to tint the leaves, we prepared to make the trip west to return Mom to her home in Sumner. A hint of melancholy filled the air when we had to give her up. She didn't seem to mind. She had things to do before the winds of winter began to blow.

Flo was a woman who believed in being prepared for all contingencies. Before these back-to-Illinois treks, she insisted I pick up fresh batteries for the small flashlight she carried in her purse. "My flashlight might come in handy if a fuse blows and the lights go out on the car. It never hurts to be prepared," she told me.

Being prepared was her motto. Perhaps that was one reason she did such a fine job raising six children on her own. Besides batteries, she always carried her squeeze cheese and cracker supply to pass around as snacks.

After we dropped Mom off in Sumner, we set out on the return journey back to Goodview. Things didn't seem quite the same. Quiet and unassuming little Flo wasn't in the car with us. She was a distinct force for good to have with you.

The Bible says, "Charm is deceitful and beauty is passing, but a woman who fears the Lord, she shall be praised" (Prov. 31:30). Many years have passed since Flo went home to be with her Savior. When we pass on, we leave all our material possessions behind. A lot of them end up in the trash or at a yard sale. Eventually, they break or get ruined entirely. Our legacies are what we leave in the lives of the people we have known. Flo left a large legacy.

A good name lasts forever. "A good name is to be chosen rather than great riches, loving favor rather than silver and gold" (Prov. 22:1). King Solomon declared, "A good name is better than precious ointment" (Eccl. 7:1).

Florena Fiscus Zollars had a good name. I am 92 years old as I write these words, and I am still thanking God I knew her.

CHAPTER SIXTEEN

Call Doctor Sam

Summer was when we executed our planned recreational program for energetic young people who were out of school and wanted something to do besides cutting grass and pulling weeds. As with other activities, Maxine and I were in charge.

Vacation Bible School was the main event for the grammar school set, but teenagers craved excitement after spending so many days cooped up in unairconditioned classrooms waiting for the final bell, signaling the beginning of summer vacation.

In the country, we had no access to pricey, well-ventilated cottages with comfortable beds and stimulating programs run by counselors wearing monogrammed T-shirts. For us, summer meant damp tents on the hard ground down by the Roanoke River. But our teens never cared about the creature comforts. It was the adult volunteers who had to take a few days to get the kinks out when they got back home.

Jimmie Jones had a suggestion: "If you're looking for a place to slow them down, let them climb Sharp Top." Sharp Top Mountain was hard to miss. The 3,875-foot peak dominates the entire region. To make the strenuous climb or spend a day picnicking at the mountain's base required driving through the town of Bedford, the county seat about twelve miles from Goodview.

The stepping-off place for the hour-and-a-half climb to the summit was near the Peaks of Otter Lodge located on the Blue Ridge Parkway, the magnificent 469-mile-long scenic highway constructed during the Great Depression as part of President Roosevelt's New Deal. The scenery is breathtaking. Carpeted with rhododendrons and mountain laurels in June and a quilt-like tapestry of colorful foliage in the fall, the area provides stunning vistas of lakes, verdant landscapes, and far-off mountain ranges. It was the place to spend time with the young people.

The plan for the day was to climb the mountain and picnic on hotdogs, marshmallows, and buckets of potato chips. For energy-ignited teens, it was a giggly scramble to the top, with the hardiest climbers waving triumphantly from the peak while others struggled to make it up there.

Maxine reached the halfway mark before finding a bench alongside the trail and calling it quits. "I think I'll wait here until you get back," she told me. I would have joined her. But as top man, I had something to prove by making it all the way to the top. When the "race you down" challenge came from one of the teens and his buddies, I deferred. I knew my limits, and I needed a slow descent back to the picnic area.

Jimmie had been right, though. He predicted the climb up Sharp Top would slow everyone down. The food was unsophisticated but perfect. We roasted hotdogs and marshmallows on bent coat hangers over a blazing campfire;

and when we finished eating, we sang round after round of choruses.

As I looked around at the 25 or so teenagers, I knew they now were ready for what I had to say. I presented the gospel and talked about the Christian life and the important decisions they would have to make along the way. We answered individual questions, the biggest one being, "How do I know the will of God for my life?" My reply was always simple: Do the right thing today. The Christian life is a day-by-day experience. Be open to opportunities. If you try an opportunity and it fails, don't worry. The next one may be when the Lord opens the door and where He directs your life.

Over the years, the Lord used these outings and others to mold our Christian teens. Many gave their lives to Christ or rededicated themselves to Him, returning home different than when they came. And so did we.

As we pulled the last wieners from the coat hangers and were packed up and ready to leave, Maxine commented on the area's beauty and felt we would enjoy going back often. And we did exactly that for the next 50 years.

The Bedford Boys

The county seat of Bedford boasted some 3,200 residents, most of whom worked in an assortment of small industries, shops, and services. Downtown Bedford, if you could call it that, was dominated by four institutions: the courthouse, Green's Drug, Coleman's Restaurant, and the People's Bank.

The little town had all the elements for comfortable rural living, whether you stopped there for business or went to

Coleman's for a plate of southern fried chicken. But a day in June 1944 stopped everything in its tracks. That was when a Western Union teletype arrived at Green's Drug that injected such a deep state of shock into people that it still lingered when we arrived in the area in 1953.

It turns out that before World War II, many of the town's young men signed on with the National Guard. Some later said they joined for the dollar-a-day stipend and nifty uniform that attracted attention from Bedford's young ladies. When the war broke out, their unit was called to active duty and shipped off to England for the invasion of Europe. Consequently, the Bedford Boys found themselves in the force that spearheaded the June 6, 1944, attack on Omaha beach in Normandy, France.

Before the day was out, 19 of the 35 Bedford Boys had fallen to German fire on the beach. Two more lost their lives later in the Normandy campaign, and two more died elsewhere. Bedford would go down in American history as the community that proportionately suffered the severest D-Day losses. It was a distinction that wore heavily on hearts and one that would never be forgotten.

Because of Bedford's great sacrifice, the U.S. Congress designated Bedford, Virginia, as the appropriate site for the National D-Day Memorial. The magnificent monument opened on June 6, 2001, drawing people to the small Virginia town from across the nation and other lands to pay tribute to those who gave their lives in recognition of the cost of freedom.

One of the men who survived the war was a surgeon, Sam Rucker, who stepped out of the war to become a legend.

Doctor Sam

Among our many community activities was one Maxine and I never expected. We became the unofficial Goodview rescue squad and emergency ambulance service. When someone became seriously ill in the night, we were called to transport them to the hospital in Roanoke.

While I drove, Maxine sat in the back seat attending to the patient. Many folks in the village had no vehicles of their own, so it made sense for them to call us. More often, however, people called us during the day to take them to Moneta, nine miles away, to get in line at Dr. Sam Rucker's office.

Yes, get in line. When we turned in at the property on Rucker Drive, we entered a bygone century. Dr. Rucker worked out of a 10-foot by 10-foot building that isn't as big as some backyard sheds today. There was no waiting room. Every examination and procedure took place in that little office. Patients waited in cars or stood in line outside the office until their turn came. Entrance was based on an honor system—first come, first served.

Inside was the quintessential country doctor who returned home from the war to follow his father in the practice of medicine. Medicine seemed to consume Doctor Sam. He certainly wasn't concerned about making money. Often, when a patient asked him, "How much?" he would reply, "Fifty cents." When someone couldn't pay in cash, he accepted produce or something from the farm.

A typical day found him in the office until noon, and then he was off to make house calls. His father before him had done so on horseback. Sam Jr. did it in cars—wearing out so many that the townspeople contributed replacements.

Unfortunately, all his skills and those of the physicians at the hospital in Roanoke couldn't forestall the departure of Hannibal Stokes.

So Mote It Be

Hannibal Stokes's relationship to the church could best be described as occasional. Others in his family were regulars in attendance. But Hannibal was a true believer in Jesus Christ, so when he died, I expected to conduct the funeral. I was in for a surprise.

Unbeknown to me, Hannibal belonged to the Masonic Lodge. I found this fact out when I received a call from the Grand Master of the fraternity instructing me concerning the part I was to play in the graveside ceremony.

"You understand that this is a Masonic funeral," he said. "You will be asked to offer a short prayer and perhaps a few brief remarks before the service begins, after which I will be in charge."

His curt words were unambiguous. I was to be more of a spectator than a pastor. I had never attended a Masonic event, but I wasn't completely in the dark about the lodge and the conduct of affairs in the society. My father had been a member for several years but left the Masons after he had become a born-again Christian.

Dad didn't hesitate to expose some of the secrets of the secret society and delighted in giving a Masonic handshake to men he knew belonged to the organization, but he had never discussed funeral protocol with me. So, I was intrigued to see what would be involved in getting Hannibal off to the "Celestial Grand Lodge on High."

As the ritual played out, I watched in awe. Men in freshly pressed suits bearing Masonic white aprons responded with choruses of "So mote it be," meaning "Amen," to phrases often shrouded in mysticism that sounded like mumbo jumbo to me. The service was a bit eerie; and the dark secret ritual I saw depressed me.

That funeral deepened my appreciation for the clarity of Christ-centered teaching about death and resurrection and awakened in me a new appreciation for the simplicity of the gospel and the message of being in heaven with the Lord Jesus in the immediacy of death. If Jesus is our personal Lord and Savior, absent from the body is present with the Lord (2 Cor. 5:8). The instant we die, we are with Him. There's no mumbo jumbo about it.

When the inevitable arrives, we will find ourselves immediately in the arms of Christ, who said, "If I go and prepare a place for you, I will come again and receive you to Myself; that where I am, there you may be also" (Jn. 14:3). And there is no better place to be than with Jesus.

CHAPTER SEVENTEEN

The Ballad of Oink McGhee

Driving home alone after being the guest preacher at a revival meeting always provided a good time to unwind and reflect on what God had accomplished through the pulpit. This had been a very good week.

My cherished friend Jimmie Jones was now pastor of a thriving church in Princeton, West Virginia, and had invited me to speak. Even though I would be arriving home late, I knew Maxine would be up with a hot pot of coffee on the stove, waiting to hear the news about Jimmie and Audrey. I chuckled as I wondered how she would respond to the offer I had been made. It was unique for sure.

"A pig! Someone offered you a pig?"

"He sure did. It surprised me as much as it does you."

"What did you tell him?"

"I told him that I'd take it, of course. The man was a farmer who didn't have much to give in the way of money, so he offered me the best he had. It seemed to me almost like something you would read in the Bible. How could I refuse?"

"But you don't know anything about raising pigs. How will you even get it down here?"

"He said he'd build a crate for it that would fit in the back of the car. It won't be old enough to take it from its mother for a couple of weeks, and that will give me time to build a pen, which I plan to do in the woods across the road from the house. Just think of how much pork we'll have for the freezer when the time comes to have it butchered," I told my wife.

I wasn't completely unfamiliar with pork products. My first after-school, weekend job was at the Remus butcher shop minimart in Romulus where I learned all the pig parts from snout to ham. I was 12 years old and worked for 35 cents an hour. Not only did I become somewhat of a hand with pork, but I also learned about the market for beef, poultry, sausages, and assorted cold cuts.

As a matter of fact, I was so adept that the boss entrusted me with the poultry distribution position at the weekly Bingo games sponsored by the local Progressive Club. The top prizes were live chickens and turkeys supplied by the Remus brothers. After a night at the Bingo tables, the lucky winners showed me their winning tickets; and I'd plunge my hands into the crates and deliver the birds. Simple. How hard could it be to put a pig in a pen, feed it, and watch it grow until it was ready for the freezer?

"Just wait and see," I assured my skeptical wife. "You'll be glad I accepted the pig when chops and ham are on the table."

The Runt

Being a first-time pastor means there are a lot of things you don't know a lot about—things never taught in seminary. My pig, affectionately named Oink McGhee, was one of them.

After a few weeks of filling the trough with table scraps

and bags of grain that I hauled in from the feed store, I noticed Oink wasn't growing much. *Well, okay*, I thought. *Maybe this is normal.* When things didn't improve over time, I decided to seek expert advice. My confidant was Lewis, a man with a large farm and a lot of pigs.

An amateur vet, Lewis took a long, hard look at Oink; picked him up for closer inspection; then began to smile. "Preacher," he told me, "that man gave you the runt of the litter. It doesn't matter how much you feed it, don't ever expect it to grow to be hog-sized."

When Maxine and I sat down to enjoy our time together that evening, I asked her, "Do you think that man knew he was giving me the runt of the litter?"

"Well, here is another consideration," she replied, smiling. "Perhaps he listened to your preaching, didn't like what he heard, and decided to get even."

I thought she might be on to something. Nevertheless, money was tight, and Oink came in handy around Thanksgiving when he became food for our table. As I disassembled McGhee's pen, my mind ambled through what I might learn from the failed venture. It was this: Perhaps finding your fit in life is a process of elimination. Try everything reasonable; and if you fail as abjectly as I had with my oinker, cross it off as one less thing to try again. I was done raising pigs. My next failure would involve agriculture.

Uncle Claude and Kentucky Wonders

I came from a long line of gardeners. My father and his four brothers all worked in industry to support their families, but that's not what they talked about on warm spring weekends when they got together. They talked about planting: who would plant what and which one would outdo the others in produce production. Even as a youngster, I noticed the competition.

Who actually planted, nurtured, and harvested the best crop was debatable, but the man who talked the best garden was Uncle Claude. Uncle Claude topped my uncle list. A severe asthmatic, we often found him in a smoke-filled room heavy with the smell of Asthmador, a fine powder he inhaled for temporary relief of an asthma attack.

No one could tell a story like Uncle Claude, and he loved to regale us youngsters with his Uncle Remus-like tales. They enthralled us. Some of the relatives who were less inclined to appreciate a foray into fantasy to escape the daily drudgery scoffed that it was the Irish in him that enabled him to bend the truth so artfully. Admittedly, my uncle specialized in embellishment. And the more he told us the same story, the better it became.

Like his siblings (my father included), Uncle Claude enjoyed turning loamy rich Michigan soil into vegetable beds. Although his medical condition restricted him and he couldn't work hard enough to make his garden outshine or even match the others in size, he never lacked a story about the superiority of his little patch.

I remember one morning when my brothers, Walter and Kenneth, and I found our uncle leaning back in a padded rocking chair on his front porch. "I'm glad to see you boys," he said in a somewhat subdued tone. "Your old uncle has had a bad night of it. You know how hot and sticky it was yesterday. Well, what made it worse," he continued, "was that I had to get up in the middle of the night and close my window. Those Kentucky Wonder beans I planted yesterday afternoon were making so much noise popping out of the ground I had to close the window to try and get at least some sleep."

The man couldn't help himself. Even though illness was overtaking him, his imagination and determination to have a story for us despite how bad he felt won the day. I've forgotten much about my other uncles, but I've never forgotten the storyteller.

I wonder what Uncle Claude what have to say about this? I thought, as I surveyed my pitiful garden in Goodview. Whereas others in town grew wonderful delicacies, I didn't. But my pathetic little vegetable patch would have produced many a colorful tale for my dear Uncle Claude.

I suppose the garden is a good illustration for a bit of spiritual truth: It's not important how big your garden grows but how faithfully you tend it. God doesn't necessarily call us to get results. He calls us to be faithful in sowing the seed and watering the soil. The results are up to Him.

When God called the prophet Ezekiel to preach, He told him, "I am sending you to the children of Israel. . . . Whether they hear or whether they refuse, . . . they will know that a prophet has been among them" (Ezek. 2:3, 5). Scripture doesn't tell us if Ezekiel ever made a difference to the people of Israel. But when the prophet got to heaven, I have no doubt he heard the words we all want to hear: "Well done, good and faithful servant" (Mt. 25:21).

I don't know what Uncle Claude would have said about my garden. But when I see him in heaven, I'll ask him.

CHAPTER EIGHTEEN

The World Pays a Visit

Missions week held a cherished spot on the Goodview Baptist Church calendar. During those eight days, the world visited our small hamlet in the hills.

Missionaries from a variety of agencies who were on furlough from their fields of service brought news to us of what was taking place far away and how God was working in hearts. With the missionaries also came colorful displays from the countries they represented, along with various small items from their fields that often became take-home gifts for our parishioners.

As was the standard of the day, the missionary families stayed in the homes of church members who relished the opportunity to hear stories from distant lands. These pairings frequently generated relationships that lasted far beyond the conference. Genuine friendships developed that enhanced and intensified the church's interest in and commitment to worldwide missions.

For Maxine, missions week produced pleasant interludes with time to sip tea with other women who bore the same responsibilities abroad that she bore in the States. She even was taken aback a bit when one missionary commented that she had a much nicer home in Africa than the one we lived in near the dusty Goodview thoroughfare.

In the decade of the 1950s, missions week also brought reports of the price some people paid when they answered the call to bring the gospel to other lands.

Remembering the Martyrs

In January 1956, five young men—Jim Elliot, Nate Saint, Peter Fleming, Ed McCully, and Roger Youderian—moved themselves and their families into one of the most hostile tribal areas in the rain forest of southern Ecuador. Their base was situated near a dangerous Indian tribe known then as the Aucas, one of the most violent groups of people in the region.

Their plan was to fly over the village, dropping gifts in a bucket. After a few days, the Auca men were smiling and returning small gifts to the missionaries in the plane. Thinking it safe to make contact, the men landed their plane on January 7 on a stretch of beach by the river. The next day, Auca men speared all five of them to death.

The murders sent shock waves the world over and stunned Christians, awakening within them a new, more vibrant commitment to world missions than had been witnessed in years. Jim Elliot's immortal words have since embedded themselves into the American-Christian psyche: "He is no fool who gives what he cannot keep to gain that which he cannot lose."

Decades earlier, the Lord had used Oswald J. Smith, the renowned founding pastor of The Peoples Church in

Toronto, Canada, to move a generation to reassess its view of world missions. "Why should anyone hear the gospel twice," he asked, "before everyone has heard it once?"

Witnesses to the Dark Years

Many of the young men in the pews during our missions week had fought through the horrific struggles of World War II. The Nazis' genocidal crimes against humanity were fresh in the minds of believers in those days.

Jimmie Jones, who directed our missions program before leaving to pastor a church of his own, endured the Battle of the Bulge, where 89,000 American soldiers were wounded and 19,000 killed. It was one of the bloodiest battles in the war. Two of our young veterans helped liberate the Nazi death camps that Adolf Hitler built to exterminate the Jewish people.

Today, the world is rife with Holocaust deniers. But no one denied the Holocaust then. Too many had witnessed the awful truth with their own eyes.

As the missionaries presented their reports, we sensed their profound love and passion for the people to whom they ministered. And though they were happy to be here in the States visiting family and their supporting churches, they longed to get back to their people on the field.

As far as I was concerned, it was the representatives from the Jewish agencies that tugged most at my heart. They conveyed something the other representatives could not. The ravages of the Holocaust were but a few short years behind them. And every single one of them had lost family members or friends to Hitler's killing machine. They knew firsthand what it was like to be persecuted simply because they were Jewish. And along with those memories, they held a burning desire to share the knowledge of Messiah Jesus, whom they had come to love.

As we listened, Maxine and I wondered why we didn't know more about what the Jewish people had suffered during the war. I had heard little or nothing about it. I found out later our Western leaders had information about the atrocities and genocide but felt they had larger issues to address.

After the war, when the numbers emerged, the world learned the horrific magnitude of the Nazi slaughter: Six million innocent Jewish men, women, and children perished. Yes, perhaps there had been other issues to address, but certainly one of the largest was that a war had been waged against the Jewish people that annihilated one-third of the world's Jewish population.

The Call to Send the Light

When we stood to sing our last anthem calling us to send the light of Jesus into the world, Maxine and I found ourselves asking, "Should we go? What should we do?" The issue was very much on our minds as we walked across the grass to the parsonage.

"Do you think we should leave here and offer ourselves to become missionaries?" I asked. We gave the thought serious prayer over the next few days. I was still very young in the ministry and had a great deal to learn. And my people at Goodview were well equipped to teach me. So we felt, for the time being, that I would stay at Goodview. But the Lord used that conference to give me a deep love and burden for the Jewish people that would never leave me.

About twenty years later, when I was pastoring my fourth church, I became friends with Dr. Victor Buksbazen and his wife, Lydia, who were Jewish believers and supported missionaries. They drove from church to church speaking to believers about the need to carry the gospel to the Jewish people. Victor was the executive director of The Friends of Israel Gospel Ministry, a worldwide, evangelical Christian organization that loves Israel and strives to see that Jewish people have access to the gospel so that they can learn who Jesus is and how much He loves them.

Lydia was a wonderful communicator. Victor was quieter than his wife and was an academic who spoke multiple languages. Both were gracious and refined; and they infused something into my life that God later would use to alter the course of my work and lead me into Jewish missions.

CHAPTER NINETEEN

Changing Places

I had been in Goodview six years when my friend Jim Elkins and his family came to visit. Jim talked to us about leaving Virginia and taking a church in Chicago. In fact, he had recommended me to the pulpit committee of the Tabernacle Baptist Church.

I already felt the Lord was bringing my work in Goodview to a close, and a move to Chicago made a lot of sense. If I pastored there, I could further my education at Moody Bible Institute.

"It would be a good fit for you," Jim said. "It's a historic church with plans to relocate somewhere in the suburbs. With the experience you have had, it would be a place to continue to grow and lead a congregation with a solid group of young couples you and Maxine could relate to. Furthermore, there's a lot going on in Chicago that I know would appeal to you."

Chicago, in fact, was not new to me. My family lived there for more than a year during the war while my father worked for the Howard Aircraft Company. On the one hand, I knew Jim was correct. I'd have more opportunities for ministry and further study. But on the other hand, having been raised near Detroit, I wasn't enthused about life in the city.

True, Maxine and I both would be closer to our mothers in the Midwest. Sumner was only fifty miles from Chicago, and my mom was about three hours away. Neither of them was getting any younger, so being available in case of emergencies or prolonged illnesses seemed a consideration.

God's will, or ours? We didn't know. After I went to Chicago for a week to see what the church had to offer, the pulpit committee extended a call for me to become the pastor. All the potential positives attracted us, but two issues needed to be settled before we could make a final decision.

First, was Chicago the Lord's will? Second, if it was, how could we be certain of it?

Although new to the business of making major changes of direction in our service for Christ, we understood that ministry wasn't about looking for a better offer. It was all about being in the place of God's choosing and in the center of God's will. Without a doubt, Goodview was God's choice for my initial years as pastor. Was He now moving us? We wanted to know for sure before we packed up and left.

We knew it would be difficult saying goodbye to the people we had served and loved for six years. That is the emotionally heavy hit a pastor takes when it is time to leave a congregation and move. Goodview had filled us with happy memories. I learned so much from the people God surrounded me with—things that never could be taught in school. Goodview was my school, and the simple, honest relationships God blessed me with there helped me grow and have stayed with me throughout my life.

The experience of building the new parsonage; seeing the many new converts and families come into the church; and the revivals, weddings, and spiritual growth we witnessed all bonded us to the people there so intensely we felt like they were blood relatives.

Maxine was especially torn by the thought of moving. "I can't make up my mind about going to Chicago. I know it will be a step up for your ministry. But I'm not thrilled with being in the city or leaving Goodview," she told me.

"Well, frankly, I'm not sure about it either," I said. "It will be a big change, and although it seems like a good thing in many ways, there are still questions."

"Why don't you talk to Morrie about it? He always gives you good advice."

She was right. So I called my buddy Morrie (Morris) Brodsky. We had become close friends since the days when he recommended me for a job in the shoe department at Sears. Morrie was well versed in knowledge of Chicago. He had graduated from Moody Bible Institute and began selling used books to Moody students, eventually growing the business into the prestigious Scripture Truth Book Company.

For years, he tried to make a respectable golfer out of me, but I was no more successful at golf than I was at selling shoes. In 1973, I wrote my first book, *The Suffering and the Glory of Israel,* on an old typewriter while sitting at Morrie's kitchen table.

When I called, Morrie suggested we meet at the Bedford golf course and make a day of it while we talked about the possibility of my moving to the Windy City. Of all the things we discussed, two of his statements stuck in my mind.

"I hate to leave when things are going so well," I confided.

"That's the point," my friend replied. "If the Lord is directing you toward a new ministry, the time to do it is when things are going well, not when there are unresolved problems to be left behind. Leaving problems isn't fair to the new pastor. He'll need time to get adjusted to the ministry without being burdened with clean-up issues."

His next comment bore something of a prophetic tone that I would remember repeatedly over my many years of ministry. "Elwood," he said, "I'm convinced that the Lord lays out His plan for our lives and His work in stages. Every stage prepares us for another. In other words, we are in a constant state of growth.

"What you must remember is this: Get all the advice and counsel you feel you need, but when it's time to make a change, it's between you and the Lord. There may be times when friends and even members of your own family won't agree with a decision that to them may seem a tad radical. Their advice will always be related to your first reservation: If things are going well, stay put. Why make a change after all the time and effort you put into a work?

"But if you think about it, that's a secular point of view. Being in ministry for the right reasons is not all about your comfort. It's about His will and accomplishing what He has fashioned you for."

Before we parted that day, Morrie had a few more words for his fairway-trudging companion. "If you do go to Chicago, know that I'll sorely miss beating you at golf."

We both knew what he was saying. *God moves in a mysterious way, His wonders to perform.* When famed English poet William Cowper penned that hymn, he wrote from firsthand experience. I had firsthand experience as well. Cowper's words reminded me of the night on Brushy Creek Road when a young woman's prayer for someone to come and show her and her brother how to be saved got answered immediately when Jim Thomason and I knocked on her door.

I saw His mysterious way again when I walked through the door of the parsonage after meeting with Morrie and was greeted by my dear wife, whose first words were, "When do we leave?" It seemed amazing. Before I left to meet Morrie that morning, Maxine and I both seriously questioned the wisdom of leaving Goodview. But the Lord confirmed to both of us independently that it was the course for us to take. No more doubts. Now was the time to take another step in carrying out our commission in ministry.

Charlie Jones

Parting from those you have grown to know and love in the faith is a wrenching experience. If the relationship between a pastor and his people is a good one, the congregation's initial reaction is, "Why? What have we done to make you want to leave us?" The situation was especially traumatic for us because this was our first experience leaving a church we had shepherded. Goodview was where we began to grow and learn how to function in a pastoral ministry.

But with time and many personal conversations conducted during covered-dish departure dinners, we all grew more comfortable with the inevitability of the situation. Change is always difficult. But when God is in it, He makes the transitions easier, as He did at Goodview.

"Where do we look for a man to take your place?" people

wanted to know. It was a question I couldn't answer because I didn't feel it wise for a departing preacher to participate in selecting his successor. That was a job for a properly appointed church committee. As it turned out, the Lord already made His choice, and the right man was close at hand. He had visited Maxine and me at the church many times, and people liked him.

I first met Charlie (Charles) Jones through events sponsored by the Salem Baptist Church and Piedmont Bible College in Winston-Salem, North Carolina. Charlie was a Piedmont graduate, and we soon forged a friendship through a common interest. Charlie had a magnificent voice and a fascination with the ballads that British, Scottish, and Scot Irish immigrants brought to the Appalachian Mountains.

These story-filled songs told of the weariness and woes afflicting the people carving out homesteads in the wilderness. Interestingly, woven into most of these renditions was a plea to the God of providence to help them endure the rigors of daily deprivation and hardship. And though the theology sometimes lacked coherence, the cries were heartfelt. The first time I heard Charlie sing the 19th-century song *Wayfaring Stranger,* it struck a chord deep within me.

I'm just a poor wayfaring stranger
Traveling thru this world below.
There's no sickness, no toil, no danger
In that bright land to which I go.
I'm going there to see my father
And all my loved one's who've gone on.
I'm just going over Jordan
I'm just going over home.

The message in the African American spirituals intrigued me in the same way. The common thread was a struggle for survival and the need for heaven—for that better place of rest, reunion with family who went on ahead, and the presence of the Savior who loved them and gave them hope. Many of the songs were born out of an era when people were illiterate and learned about God and heaven through music.

Though the desperation expressed in these cries was slipping away from a nation steeped in excessive wealth and comfort, the need for God remained. The driving force in preaching the gospel had not diminished. The gospel's simplicity compounds its divine power. That fact has never changed, and my friend understood it. The people of Goodview Baptist understood as well. For them, the gospel had altered the spiritual face of their community. Therefore, their foremost question to a prospective candidate for their pulpit was the same question they asked me when I was a candidate: "Do you faithfully preach the gospel and provide an invitation for people to accept Christ as their personal Savior?"

"Do you think Reverend Jones would consider becoming a candidate for pastor?" the board chairman asked me.

"I don't know. Why don't you ask him and see if he would be interested."

So, they asked. When Charlie answered yes, I was relieved. Goodview Baptist could not have found a better man for its pulpit. Charlie had preached at the church many times when he and his wife, Emma, visited us. In addition to his musical gifts and excellent preaching skills, Charlie was a people person—a quality that endeared him quickly to the rural congregation.

With the unanimous consent of the membership, Charlie would step into the pastorate to begin his tenure in concert with our departure. Our hearts and minds were at peace. We would leave with the assurance that our beloved people were well cared for.

Honeysuckle and Coconut Cake

"What do you think you'll miss most when we leave?" I asked Maxine as we reminisced about our years in Goodview.

"Odd you should ask that," she replied. "And odd what has come to my mind. Of course, I'll miss the people. We have so many good memories of everything we experienced. But I can't help remembering those long rides we took during the summer when the honeysuckle bushes covered the fences along the road. Every time we did it, it brought back memories of when I was a child and Mom would open the window next to our beds so we could smell the honeysuckle that grew outside.

"Then there is Doris Thomason's wonderful coconut cake that I'm going to miss so much. No one will ever make a cake that compares to hers. But there is something else about that memory that sticks in my mind. When we first came here— before we had water in the house—I was carrying buckets from the spring into the kitchen. I can see Jim on his knees, hooking up the pump and piping that would relieve me of that awful job. Then there is everything else he and Doris did for us without our ever having to ask. That was what we found here with these people that I will miss terribly. And it makes me wonder if we'll ever find it again."

"What I think about," I said, "is how little we knew when

we arrived, and how very much we're taking away. I don't think we'll ever find a place where the people are like these Goodview folk. In one way, things have been simple—away from the crush of life in crowded places. I guess what I'm trying to say is that life here has no hurry about it, which gave us the time necessary to absorb a dimension of practical ministry that I don't think we'll find time for in the city."

We absorbed so much in Goodview. Because I was the only pastor, I did everything; and people shared their lives with us—their joys, their sorrows, their griefs. They knocked on the door at midnight when they were sick, and Maxine and I were there for them. I learned how to minister to people's needs, how to sit with them and comfort them when they were dying and how to rejoice when them when they married off their children.

Their decent, hard-working, simple values permeated everything they did. God had sovereignly placed me into this environment at this particular time because He knew it was exactly what I needed after being saturated with theory and theology in school. I needed real people. Real life. I needed to sit with the Daniels sisters, rocking away on their front porch as they told me how desperately they wanted to see their brother saved. I needed Jim Thomason and Jimmie Jones, true servants of Christ whose help and friendship showed me what it means to be a faithful, God-honoring Christian. I needed all the experiences Goodview provided to show me that trusting God is always the way to go, even when that path leads you to do what others consider illogical.

I could have gone to a big church, where I would have had fewer responsibilities as part of a church staff. But I turned that position down to become the pastor and chief cook and bottle washer at Goodview. And neither Maxine nor I ever regretted it.

When I gave my life to Christ, I got down on my knees, repented of my sin, and stood up a son of God. There is no substitute for the richness of being in His hand.

"About that honeysuckle," I told Maxine. "If you feel a burst of deprivation from the invigorating scent you so cherish, it will only take a little over an hour to get down to Sumner and sit near the bush by your bedroom window. As for Doris's coconut cake, now that we'll be so far away, maybe you can coax that secret recipe out of her so you can try your hand at making one of your own."

Those were issues to ponder another time. We both knew tomorrow would be a very long day.

CHAPTER TWENTY

Saying Goodbye

We sat outside for a long time our last evening in Goodview. It was a lovely night, and we could see the moon rising from the east far across the fields. We didn't say much to each other as we sat there together. Finally, Maxine broke the silence.

"I thought I was prepared for this, but I'm not. Every time I think about these people and parting from them, I tear up."

"Well," I replied, "I think that's normal. After all, we've been together so long. And they've become like family to us."

"I know. And that's what makes it hard. Some of them will come by in the morning to see us off. And I just don't know if I can handle it."

"That's one reason to leave very early," I replied.

When You're Sure You're Lost . . .

"Strange," said Maxine. "But I've been thinking about what Pastor Yeatts told us before we came. Do you remember?"

"I do. When you're sure you're lost, you're almost there."

"When we came around that seemingly endless mountain road and began to discuss the possibility of being lost," she said, "suddenly, there was Goodview! At that moment it was just a place to us—a little hamlet that filled us with expectation. And we weren't disappointed.

"But lately, I've been thinking about those words in another way. It's about all those people who responded to the gospel or had their lives transformed in other ways. Because it's true; people never come to Christ as their Savior until they're sure they're lost.

"A perfect example was Tommy, the blacksmith. Remember how many times he put you off saying he wasn't going to attend church until he could make his life better? It wasn't until he realized he couldn't make his life better without Jesus that he became sure he was lost—which meant he was almost there."

"Which makes me think," I said, "of the simplicity of the gospel message and how many people we have seen that message change."

Early the next morning the movers loaded the last of our belongings into a truck and left for Chicago.

We said our goodbyes and started down the dusty road past the banks of fenced honeysuckles and fields of meandering cattle toward the highway. It seemed strange to be looking at what we were leaving behind through the rearview mirror. But Chicago awaited, and we were ready to move on to the next chapter in our ministry.

Maxine

CHAPTER TWENTY-ONE

Maxine

On any warm, sunny afternoon in the mid 1930s, porch sitters along Carey Street in Sumner, Illinois, would see the Zollars girl wearing out her strap-on roller skates as she crisscrossed the smooth sidewalks in town. There were no strangers among the people she waved to along her route in a hometown that typified small-town America, where life was pleasantly predictable.

The setting was dramatically different some twenty-five years later when she addressed a question posed by a woman at a luncheon. "And what is it as a pastor's wife that you actually do?" Maxine did a million things. But all she said in reply was, "I look after my husband, then do what I feel the Lord wants of me in the church and community."

My late friend Dr. Fred Brown once said, "Any preacher who doesn't have the good sense to marry above himself isn't worth his salt." In that case, I must be worth my salt.

Fred's comment reflected the essence of the Lord's Word when He initiated the institution of marriage at the dawn of the human experience. "Then the LORD God said, 'It is not good for the man to be alone; I will make him a helper suitable for him'" (Gen. 2:18, NASB).

A "suitable" woman crafted for a specific man. Nothing complicated about it when God does the choosing. For me, He chose the skater from across the Wabash in southern Illinois, a woman with the virtue of knowing what it took to keep a man together. She was an asset to the ministry in a way that no one else was qualified to be.

Being a wife and mother is a lifelong occupation, let alone being a busy pastor's wife. It was always Mom who did the final inspection to see her boy had on a clean shirt and pressed corduroys before leaving for school.

I was reminded of how little those things change when I spoke at a conference in Florida. As I left my room, two women approached me, smiling broadly. "Your wife isn't with you?" one of them asked.

"No," I replied, wondering why she would pose such a question.

"We thought so," she said. "No woman in her right mind would allow you out of your room wearing that tie with the color shirt you have on."

My "suitable" life mate was the perfect fit. In ability, she was multidimensional; in person, compassionate; in discernment, perceptive; in practical matters, imbued with common sense; in relationships, loyal; in controversies, frank but fair.

Her preparation for Goodview was the school of the Great Depression, where she learned by observation the art of making do. She knew how to provide the appearance of plenty when little existed to validate the illusion. Even today, our children think her fried baloney constituted a spectacular dining experience.

Although she was extremely personable and well-liked, most people—even those who knew her well—thought of Maxine as Mrs. McQuaid. I suppose her demeanor defined her. Hers was a generation that dressed for the occasion. Saturday shopping required dresses and hats, not jeans and flipflops. Sunday was a step above Saturday. Even though she followed the code of outward propriety, it was my good fortune to have married a genuine lady.

Her Legacy in Letter

On September 12, 2016, the Lord called Maxine home. While going through some of her things after she was taken from us, I came across a piece she had written and tucked away. As I read it, it struck me that I was reading her legacy—what she cherished and was bequeathing to those of us she left behind:

> *At this Thanksgiving time, I'm counting my blessings. I'll start with having a wonderful mother, brothers, and sisters. I thank the Lord for causing me even as a ten-year-old girl to want to know the true way of salvation. I'm thankful for my father-in-law who was faithful in telling me the way of salvation and leading me and Elwood to the Lord in 1948. I'm thankful for how the Lord has cared for us so wonderfully and faithfully over all these years. I'm thankful to see all our children grown and my grandchildren, and now*

even my great-grandchildren, well and strong. The Lord has blessed us so much more than I could ever ask for or deserve.

When the Lord comes back in the clouds to call all His saved ones, my most fervent prayer is that all my family will meet me in the air so we can all arrive in heaven together. Thank you, Lord, for everyone and everything you have blessed me with.

I, too, am waiting for the day when we all will be together with the Lord, and I will see Maxine again. "For the Lord himself shall descend from heaven with a shout, with the voice of the archangel, and with the trump of God: and the dead in Christ shall rise first: Then we which are alive and remain shall be caught up together with them in the clouds, to meet the Lord in the air: and so shall we ever be with the Lord" (1 Th. 4:16–17).

EPILOGUE

It's difficult to leave a place where the people have unconsciously been your mentors and become such a large part of what you are. Although I have been away from the quaint rural island of a generation we discovered among the rolling hills of Virginia seventy years ago, neither the place nor the people have left my heart or mind.

Goodview and a thriving Goodview Baptist Church still exist. But virtually everyone we knew there all those years ago is gone. I don't know whether people of the sort who lived up and down the hills and hollows of Goodview and similar rural villages can be found anywhere now.

That quality of life and stability of values have all but disappeared. Today we confront a daunting, downward plunge into neopaganism. Is it irreversible? Only God knows. From my perspective, we need to return to the qualities that made us what we once were. Oddly enough, those virtues are best revisited, not in America's teeming metropolises, but in the small towns where ordinary folks set the standard.

Rural Goodview of the 1950s was such a place—a mixture of lightheartedness, common sense, and dedication influenced by a spiritual dimension that speaks to the need in each of us.

As I was working on this book, I decided to return there to visit an area beyond where the pavement ends. In the early days of our ministry, that meant going "across the creek" where a line of houses stood that were occupied by church members. To my surprise, decrepit relics of some small homes still stand there, as do the outlines of small, weeded gardens that once provided delicious vegetables for summer tables.

My immediate impression was how quickly things change. What we once regarded as permanent passes swiftly into history. Everything is different. The general store burned down; the railroad depot that served as the community's nerve center has long since collapsed and disappeared; and the blacksmith shop, canning factories, and sawmills all are gone. Rut-filled gravel roads that once challenged everything Mr. Firestone and his competitor tire maker, Goodyear, manufactured are also things of the past.

The greatest change for me, however, involves the Goodview Baptist Church. The original structure, built in 1922, was a picturesque, winged building with white clapboard siding on the outside and beaded wooden walls within. Air conditioning in the sweltering summers of rural Virginia was almost unknown back then, and most country folk would have scoffed at the thought anyway. They were strong people with equally strong opinions and did not think it an indignity to perspire a bit while worshiping the Lord. Hand fans supplied gratis by local undertakers stuck out of the hymnal racks along the backs of varnished wooden pews; and when waved, they moved the heavy, sultry summer air just fine.

That little church is gone now. All that remains is an etching of the old structure hanging in the vestibule of the new building. I must say, the new building, with its brick exterior, is a fine-looking house of worship. It has stylish beamed ceilings, snow-white walls, and stained glass to color the light flowing through the windows. All those funeral fans bearing pastel pictures of Bible scenes have long since vanished, replaced by whooshing gusts of cool air forced in by an up-to-date air conditioning system.

It's impossible to go "across the creek" these days. That was the route we had to use to visit half of the congregation we were called to shepherd. The creek lay in a deep depression. Currently, the road ends unceremoniously before an expanse of water that cuts the community in half. The dissection came when the Appalachian Electric Power Company built a hydroelectric dam that did away with life as we knew it during our tenure there. Goodview has since been converted into a resort area, sporting expensive homes, vacation chalets, manicured golf courses, expensive restaurants, and boats— lots of boats. The fields surrounding the lake where farmers toiled to plant and harvest crops has given way to homes for well-to-do retirees and a vast getaway playground for pleasure seekers.

The Bible says, "For what is your life? It is even a vapor that appears for a little time and then vanishes away" (Jas. 4:14). So much has changed. I miss them, those "plain people." In my younger days, I imagined they would never change, never pass, never leave this idyllic spot. But they are gone, and I have grown old. Yet I am grateful to God for the years I spent in Goodview. The people who inhabited this envelope of time left an indelible imprint on our history that will never be erased or duplicated.

Goodview was my seminary, where I received training of

a people-oriented fashion that would last my entire life. And though the Lord placed me in ministries over the years that have taken me far and wide across countless countries and places, Goodview has always been with me. And for that, I can never adequately express my gratitude.